NO MORE CHRISTIAN NICE GIRL

Books by

Paul Coughlin

FROM BETHANY HOUSE PUBLISHERS

Five Secrets Great Dads Know

Married . . . But Not Engaged (with Sandy Coughlin)

No More Christian Nice Girl (with Jennifer Degler, PhD)

No More Christian Nice Guy

No More Christian Nice Guy Study Guide

No More Jellyfish, Chickens, or Wimps

Unleashing Courageous Faith

NO MORE

WHEN JUST BEING NICE—INSTEAD OF GOOD—

CHRISTIAN

HURTS YOU, YOUR FAMILY, AND YOUR FRIENDS

NICE GIRL

Paul Coughlin &
Jennifer Degler, PhD

BETHANYHOUSE
MINNEAPOLIS, MINNESOTA

Published by Bethany House Publishers
11400 Hampshire Avenue South
Bloomington, Minnesota 55438

Bethany House Publishers is a division of
Baker Publishing Group, Grand Rapids, Michigan.

Printed in the United States of America

In keeping with biblical principles of creation stewardship, Baker Publishing Group advocates the responsible use of our natural resources. As a member of the Green Press Initiative, our company uses recycled paper when possible. The text paper of this book is comprised of 30% post-consumer waste.

green press INITIATIVE

Library of Congress Cataloging-in-Publication Data

Coughlin, Paul T.
    No more Christian nice girl : when just being nice instead of good hurts you, your family,
and your friends/ by Paul Coughlin and Jennifer D. Degler.
        p.   cm.
    Includes bibliographical references.
    Summary: "A look at how Christian women are conditioned to be falsely nice instead of
genuinely good. Shows how they can follow Jesus' example and speak the truth in love, becoming authentic, powerful women of loving faith"—Provided by publisher.
    ISBN 978-0-7642-0769-3 (pbk. : alk. paper) 1. Christian women—Religious life. 2. Chris-
tian women—Conduct of life. 3. Women—Religious aspects—Christianity. I. Degler, Jennifer D. II. Title.
    BV4527.C686   2010
    248.8'43—dc22

                                                                    2010004188

Dedication

To Ellen Friesen, who has shown Sandy and me, today and forever, what God's Good Woman really is. Thank you for your inspiring love, friendship, strength, and courage. May our daughter live up to her namesake.

—Paul

To my Balcony Women: Rebecca Mackey, Annette Bartle, Beth Degler, Carla Gassett, and Josie Degler.

—Jennifer

PAUL COUGHLIN is a former newspaper editor and is the author of numerous books. He is the founder of The Protectors, which provides values-based and faith-based solutions to the cruelty of adolescent bullying. A popular speaker at men's, women's, parenting, and anti-bullying conferences, he has appeared on *Good Morning America, Nightline, 700 Club, Focus on the Family, C-SPAN, Los Angeles Times, The New York Times, Newsweek,* and other media outlets. His anti-bullying curriculum is used throughout North America as well as England, Canada, Australia, Uganda, and South Africa. He is a frequent radio guest in Cork, Ireland.

Paul is the Boys' Varsity Soccer Coach at St. Mary's School, where he was voted Coach of the Year, and where he is also a member of the Board of Directors. He is a member of the Southern Oregon Leadership Team for SMART: Start Making A Reader Today. He and his wife, Sandy, have three teenagers and live in southern Oregon. *www.PaulCoughlin.net*

JENNIFER DEGLER, PhD, is a clinical psychologist and life coach. A frequent speaker at women's events and marriage retreats, Jennifer is known for her entertaining and engaging presentations that make audiences laugh while they learn. She counsels adults, youth, and couples at the Interfaith Counseling Center in central Kentucky. She has served as the Ethics Chair for the Kentucky Psychological Association and is a member of the American Association of Christian Counselors.

Jennifer is the founder of Creating Christian Change, a life coaching enterprise that works with clients across the country helping them to create lives they love (*www.JenniferDegler.com*). She has appeared on television, radio, and in print as an expert in life coaching, mental health, and female sexuality. She is also the creator of CWIVES, a Web site devoted to helping Christian wives understand and enhance their sexuality (*www.cwives.com*). She and her husband, Jeff, have two teenagers and live in Lexington, Kentucky.

Acknowledgments

From Paul

Thank you to Sandy Coughlin, Barb Wiedenbeck, Janet Grant, Kortland Fuqua, Dennis Hughett Jr., Traylor Lovvorn, Rick Johnson, Jeff Anderson, Ray Huett, Tina Dupree, Jeff Rush, Steve Weydert, Kelly Wieber, and Anni Jones.

From Jennifer

Thank you to the following for their invaluable support and inspiration:

Annette and Matt Bartle; Beth, Kevin, Ken, and Pat Degler; Angie and Daniel Mackey; Carla and John Gassett; Pam Seales, Rick Landon, and the therapists and clients of the Interfaith Counseling Center; Janet Grant; the Camping Buddies (satisfied?); Debi Stack; the WOW class; the Abbey of Gethsemani; J-CURP; my prayer team; and the Bethany

House team, including Kyle Duncan, Julie Smith, Brett Benson, Tim Peterson, Amanda Hall, and our insightful editor, Ellen Chalifoux.

A special thank you to:

My mom, Rebecca Mackey, for the many hours she spent categorizing the verses that demonstrate the firmer side of Jesus.

My wonderful children, Josie and Jake, and my best friend and husband, Jeff Degler.

Contents

Frustrated, Fearful, and Fake: Meet Nicole, Christian Nice Girl

"Hold on!" you might say in response to this book's title. "Why would any Christian woman in her right mind want to stop being nice?" Well, meet Nicole, a Christian Nice Girl (CNG), and slip into the passenger's seat of her life for one day. Be sure to buckle up, because when a CNG is driving, things get bumpy very fast. Life always does when a woman chooses to be *nice* instead of *good*.

CNG Nicole

BEEP, BEEP, BEEP! As the alarm clock blares, Nicole hits the Snooze button, hoping to steal a few more minutes of precious sleep. *Why am I so tired?* she wonders before remembering she spent her third late night in a row finishing her sister's taxes and her son's science fair project. After stumbling to the shower for a speedy shampoo, Nicole wraps herself in a towel and wipes the steamy mirror. *Look at those suitcases under my eyes! Time to spackle on the concealer.*

Nicole checks the clock, groans, and pokes her head out of the bathroom. "David, will you get the kids moving and pack lunches? I'm running late, and I still need to blow-dry my hair."

"Yeah, I've got time this morning, but honey, you overslept again because you're doing too much," David replies.

The telephone interrupts their conversation. David checks the caller ID. "It's Pam, and she's sure to have a problem. If you answer the phone, sweetheart, you'll be late for work."

Guilt, her constant companion, sours Nicole's stomach as she considers David's words. Ignoring Pam's call would feel like breaking the eleventh commandment: Thou shalt not say no even if thou art running late.

"David, I'm trying to be a good Christian witness for Pam. I'll make it brief."

As David shakes his head in disbelief and heads off to wake their children, Nicole hears him mutter, "Even Jesus gave people a dose of Vitamin No sometimes."

Nicole picks up the phone, hair dripping, bra straps twisted like swizzle sticks, already dreading how hard it would be to end the call quickly and still sound nice.

"Hello."

"Hi, Nicole. Listen, I know it's early, but my ex-husband and I argued last night about where the kids should go for spring break, and I need to vent."

"Well, I guess I can talk now," fibs Nicole.

She cradles the phone on her shoulder while pulling clothes out of her closet and listening with half an ear to Pam's story. She feels like a circus performer tied up in knots as she attempts to get her panty hose on without dropping the phone. Nicole's relief at having this task accomplished vanishes as her daughter comes into the bedroom and says, "Mom, you said you would quiz me on my French vocab before school. Here's my list."

Nicole covers the phone with her hand, pastes on a fake smile, and whispers to Heather, "I'm talking with Pam right now. Ask your dad."

"But you said you would, and besides, Dad's making Tyler's lunch. You know, it's almost time to leave and your hair is still wet. And did you know your panty hose have a big run?"

"I don't have time for this! Can't you see I'm busy?" snaps Nicole. "No, no, Pam, I wasn't talking to you. I'm so sorry. Go ahead: What were you saying?" Nicole motions her daughter out of the bedroom.

Heather frowns, heads for the door, and mumbles, "Why do you always have time to help everyone but me?"

Hearing the resentment in her daughter's voice worsens the sick feeling in Nicole's stomach. At this rate, she's going to need a stiff shot of Mylanta for breakfast, but Pam's voice in her ear interrupts her thoughts.

"Nicole, are you even listening to me?! I don't think you are. I'll just call someone else who really cares."

Nicole stands stunned as the dial tone rings in her ear. Nicole tries hard—to act like a nice Christian, to keep everyone happy—but her day has barely started and already two people are mad at her. This sure doesn't feel like the abundant life Jesus promised.

After getting ready in record time, Nicole herds her daughter to the car and peels out of the driveway. She mentally reviews her workday and sighs.

"Mom, are you angry at me? You're over there sighing like you're mad at me."

Nicole shakes her head. "No, I'm not angry at you."

"Well, you're driving like we're in a race or something."

"I told you, I'm not mad at you. I was just thinking about work, and how tired I am of taking up the slack for co-workers."

"Why don't you tell them to do their own work?" asks Heather.

Nicole sighs again. "I don't know. It just seems easier to do it myself. And remember, Christians are supposed to be helpful."

"If you don't stand up for yourself, they'll just keep walking all over you. It's like when Emily was telling lies about me at school. Dad told me that was like bullying and that I had to stand up to her, and it worked."

"Heather, it's not that simple for me. These are people I have to work with, so I try hard to be nice by keeping the peace and not making waves. That's what Jesus would do."

"Dad says that Jesus didn't always keep the peace or act nice. He says—"

"It's easy for your dad to say all that! He's not a woman working in a man's world!" snaps Nicole.

"Okay, I'm sorry! Why are you always so angry?"

"I am not angry! I'm just tired of having to defend being nice. Do you want me to be mean instead?"

Heather stares out the window. "Whatever. You can let me out here."

Nicole watches her daughter head toward the high school without even a backward wave. She knows she blew it—again. *How did our relationship get so strained? We used to be so close.* Nicole prays about the situation as she drives to work.

"Dear Lord, thank you for this day. Please forgive me for my sins. Please help Heather and me to get along." Nicole pauses but can't think of anything else "prayer appropriate" to say except amen. She waits to feel better, but nothing happens. She wonders why prayer seems to work for everyone but her.

When Nicole arrives at work, she tackles the budget presentation she and her co-worker Mike are making that afternoon. Mike had agreed to design the PowerPoint slides, but his e-mail yesterday said that he was "busy with other things so you will need to do the slides instead."

Shortly before lunch, her husband sends her a text message that says, "How about lunch?" Nicole quickly texts him back, saying thanks for the offer, but she has to work through lunch to finish the missing slides. She fumes, thinking how unfair it is that she has to say no to the one thing to which she would like to say yes—lunch with her husband.

Later that day, after the budget presentation to the board of directors, the CEO comments, "Excellent work, Mike and Nicole. Your slides were very helpful in explaining how the budget cuts will affect each department."

Nicole smiles, waiting for Mike to acknowledge how she rescued their slides with her last-minute push through lunch.

"Thank you very much," Mike responds. "Those slides were a bear to put together."

Nicole turns to glare at Mike, but he's already shaking hands with the departing board members. She slips out to her office, where she stews over Mike's lack of gratitude. "Mike is a liar!" Nicole grumbles to herself. And, as if her sour stomach wasn't enough, now she can feel a migraine coming on. As she searches in her purse for an aspirin, her phone rings.

"Hello, this is Nicole Chrisman."

"Nicole, this is Stephanie Malone. I just heard that you plan on slashing my department's budget. How could you tell the board of directors that the Product Design Department can handle some cutbacks? That's stupid! We are understaffed as it is!"

Nicole feels the pounding in her head jump up the Richter scale.

"Stephanie, I'm sorry, but Product Design is not the only department with minor budget cutbacks. We had to—"

"Minor? That's not what I heard! You accounting types love to get out your red pens and slash away. Well, I'm not going to stand for this.

I don't let anybody mess with me, and upper management is going to hear from me about your idiotic cutbacks!" Stephanie crashes her phone down, hurting Nicole's ear.

Nicole slumps in her chair. This has to be the worst day of her life. First, Problem Pam, then Huffy Heather, next Mike the Mooch, and now Stephanie Steamroller. Nicole can think of only one way to soothe herself—chocolate, and lots of it. She heads for the vending machines and stands there, dejectedly debating which would make her feel better, a Snickers or a Milky Way.

"Hey, Nicole, looking for a late-afternoon pick-me-up?"

Nicole turns and sees Lisa, her co-worker and fellow church member, smiling at her.

"Yes, I have had a terrible day, and chocolate seems to be the only solution."

Lisa looks concerned. "What happened?"

"Too much to tell, but the most recent was a blistering phone call from Stephanie in Product Design. She really lit into me."

"She tried that with me once. After she cooled down, I asked her to stop ripping into me when she was upset about something."

Nicole feels her dejection deepening. "I couldn't do that. Just the thought of confronting someone makes me nervous. People like Stephanie never listen anyway."

Lisa smiles gently. "Maybe not, but if you confront Stephanie, that would show her you don't appreciate people talking to you that way. You don't have to be hateful or mean when you confront her. Just be gracious but firm."

"I like the gracious part, but the firm part is hard for me. I feel like I'm not 'turning the other cheek,' like I'm not being nice."

Lisa shakes her head slowly. "Nicole, Jesus didn't mean for believers to be doormats for other people. And Jesus certainly didn't always act nice. Listen, I've got to run, but let's talk more about this later, okay?"

Nicole slowly walks back to her office, puzzling over what Lisa said. *Jesus wasn't always nice? That doesn't sound right. Have I missed something?* As she collapses into her office chair, a familiar frustration and sadness spread inside Nicole. Nothing is working out for her like it is supposed to, no matter how hard she tries. She believes being nice will get her what she wants—better relationships, job promotions, spiritual connection—but instead people are mad at her, she's overlooked at work, and God feels a million miles away.

Nicole briefly wonders if she should try running over the top of people to get what she wants, like Stephanie does, but deep in her heart, she knows being a jerk isn't the answer. *I don't even know how I ended up this way,* Nicole thinks. *And if I'm not supposed to act nice as a Christian, then how am I supposed to behave? Why can't I get it right? I just feel stuck and stupid. And all I'm doing is trying to be nice!*

The Hard Truth About Acting Nice

Can you relate to Nicole? Perhaps when reading her story, you were reminded of yourself or another woman you care about. Far too many Christian women struggle with the same anxiety, frustration, and resentment as Nicole because they believe when dealing with life's obstacles, their only two choices are (1) act like Nice Nicole, or (2) be overbearing like Steamroller Stephanie. And choice number two isn't really an option—who wants to be mean and obnoxious? So what's left? Sadly, just choice number one: Act nice, even if it hurts you and those you love.

We know about this destructive choice firsthand because we both earn our living helping nice Christians grow into good Christians. As the author of *No More Christian Nice Guy;* founder of The Protectors, the faith-based solution to adolescent bullying; international speaker; and boys' varsity soccer coach, I (Paul) struggled with the Christian

Nice Guy problem for most of my life. It was the monkey on my back that hurt my faith, limited my ability to provide for my family, and soured my marriage for too many years. But I eventually confronted the forces that sold me the Nice Christian fallacy, and now I am sharing these hard-fought insights with you.

As a clinical psychologist and life coach, I (Jennifer) have found that the Christian Nice Girl fallacy has clipped the wings of the majority of my female clients. Like them, I have struggled to resist the "act nice" urge, even while knowing it's not good for me or others. The women I counsel who share this struggle are intelligent and caring, but they yearn for a more abundant life, both for themselves and their families and friends. And when they're really honest, they think they're going a little crazy. That's what exhaustion and following the wrong road map in life does to you.

If you want amazing changes in your life, here's our straightforward message: A lot of what people call nice behavior is really fear, cowardice, and even sin in disguise. Many women are nice not because they truly care about other people, but because they fear conflict and rejection. That's not peacemaking. That's peace-faking, and their God-given consciences have been telling them this truth for a long time. The "disease to please" runs rampant in society and in many churches, resulting in women who act more like girls than powerful women of loving faith. Consequently, far too many women are not being transformed into the true image of Christ, and not living like the heroic women of faith in the Bible. Instead, they have become hamster-wheel women of immense frustration, burnout, and depression with lives that lack purpose and integrity.

Getting a Definitive Diagnosis

Wondering if you are a Christian Nice Girl? Next is a self-test that will help you identify if the CNG problem is infecting your life. Try not to overanalyze the questions. Just go with your first, instinctive response.

SPIRITUAL AND CHURCH LIFE

True   False   Anger and conflict just seem wrong to me, like they are sins.

True   False   I am confused by or avoid discussing the parts of the Bible where Jesus isn't nice (e.g., overturning money changers' tables, calling Pharisees "white-washed tombs").

True   False   If I ask myself "WWJD," I assume he would have a gentle response.

True   False   A Christian woman should always have a smile on her face.

True   False   I probably do too much at church. (Or my family complains that I do too much at church.)

True   False   It would be wrong for me, as a Christian woman, to ever question my church staff about their beliefs, choices, actions, etc.

True   False   I feel like other women are usually closer to God than I am, and like I just can't seem to get it right spiritually.

True   False   I hide my flaws and struggles from other Christians, particularly other women.

True   False   I would ask for prayer for sick friends, but I won't ask for prayer for myself, particularly about a personal issue.

True   False   Praying about my sexuality seems weird.

RELATIONSHIPS

True   False   I've gotten burned trying to help a needy person.

True   False   I probably ask too many people for their opinions before I make a decision.

True   False   If someone gets mad at me, I usually apologize even if I don't think I've done anything wrong.

True   False   It's hard for me to ask other people for what I need.

True   False   It's better to lie to someone than to hurt his/her feelings with the truth.

True   False   I feel guilty when I say no or set firm boundaries with others.

True	False	I am very uncomfortable discussing sex (even with my husband).
True	False	My boyfriend or husband or close friend calls me names or puts me down.
True	False	I am not good at confrontations and avoid them as long as possible.
True	False	Sometimes I think that if people knew the real me, they wouldn't like me.

WORK (CAN BE PAID OR VOLUNTEER WORK, OUTSIDE OR INSIDE THE HOME)

True	False	I know I make less money than most people doing my job would earn.
True	False	Other people have told me I'm too soft-spoken at work.
True	False	Somehow I seem to end up working for abusive bosses.
True	False	My co-workers tend to dump their work on me.
True	False	I will back down rather than make waves (at work, home, or church) because I would hate to be seen as a pushy or complaining woman.
True	False	The people I supervise probably think I'm a bit of a pushover.
True	False	If given the choice, I'll play it safe instead of taking a calculated risk.
True	False	I usually volunteer to get coffee, make copies, take notes, etc., at meetings and leave the talking to others.
True	False	I feel guilty for taking scheduled breaks or sick days at work.
True	False	It's hard for me to accept compliments or take credit for a job well done.

LIFE IN GENERAL

True	False	People tell me I'm too hard on myself.
True	False	I feel selfish for having my own wants and desires.
True	False	Avoiding conflict leads to a better life.

True	False	Fear keeps me from moving ahead in life.
True	False	If I make a mistake, even if it's no big deal, I will either cover it up or apologize profusely/try to explain too much about my error.
True	False	Even if I don't like what's happening to me, I will smile my way through it and then fume or complain later.
True	False	My health suffers if I know someone is disappointed or angry with me (e.g., headaches, nausea, insomnia, diarrhea, etc.)
True	False	Even though it was unwise, I've financially helped someone because it was too hard to say no to him/her.
True	False	I am more irritable and dissatisfied than most people would guess.
True	False	I wish people would just figure out what I need without my having to directly ask for it.

Now go back and total your number of true responses. If you have five to nine true responses, you have the early stages of Nice Girliosis, and it may get worse if you don't take action now. If you answered true to ten or more questions, the Nice Girl problem has spread and needs immediate intervention, so keep reading (the laundry can wait!). Your next step after diagnosing Nice Girliosis is to figure out how you ended up with this condition and what to do about it.[1] We'll discuss these things and much more in the chapters to come, including the three common factors that, individually or in combination, can cause Christian women to act like Nice Girls instead of God's Good Women:

(1) Having an incomplete image of Jesus that focuses on his sweet side and ignores his forceful side;

(2) Giving in to the immense pressure society puts on women to hide their true selves behind a façade of niceness;

(3) Encountering harmful childhood experiences, such as lacking inspiring words or role models, having anxious parents, or suffering abuse.

We'll also look at God's Good Women of the Bible and show you how to emulate their examples. (No, they were not always sugar and spice. These women were downright spunky.) Fresh life will be breathed into your faith as you see how these godly, strong women flexed their muscles of faith and chose to be good instead of nice. As a result, they discovered how amazingly useful Christianity is in everyday life, and you can too.

We'll uncover how "acting nice" *appears* to make friendships easier—right up until it ruins those relationships and leaves you feeling used and bitter. We'll reveal how Christian Nice Girls are a magnet for Mr. Wrong, and how to date Mr. Right instead. If you're already married, there's a whole chapter to show you how to prevent the Nice Wife problem from poisoning your marriage. You might even blush as you read a frank and fun discussion about how acting nice prevents you from fully embracing and expressing your sexuality. (That's chapter 8 for those of you who want to go directly there!)

We hope light bulbs will go on for you as you realize how being a Nice Girl at work diminishes your chances for advancement and destroys the trust and respect others have for you (not to mention your own self-respect). You'll learn how to handle sticky situations at work, church, and home with graceful firmness and greater self-confidence.

After all the bad news, you'll get the great news: There is hope for Christian Nice Girls and a way out of their frustrating, fearful, and fake world. You'll get the road map for the journey from Christian Nice Girl to God's Good Woman so that you can courageously walk with integrity and purpose as you enjoy the abundant life God has planned for you. When you say good-bye to nice and hello to being God's Good Woman, you will warmly welcome the new you—authentic, energized, and level-headed (your family will greatly appreciate the last quality—no more explosions that seem to come out of nowhere).

We've included study questions at the end of each chapter, and we encourage you to write down your answers in a journal or note-book and apply this material to your life. Or join with a few others to discuss the book together. The journey is always easier when you share it with friends.

Intrigued enough to keep reading? That's good, because the next chapter is definitely an eye opener. Please turn the page and meet the real Jesus Christ—and he is much more than just meek and mild.

Study Questions

1. What parts of Nicole's day can you relate to?

2. Nicole's "disease to please" leaves her feeling tired, guilty, irritable, resentful, dejected, frustrated, confused, and sad. Do you frequently feel any of these? What is making you feel that way?

3. What impact has acting nice had on your life?

4. Review your self-test. In what areas do you struggle the most with Nice Girliosis?

   * Spiritual and church life
   * Relationships
   * Work
   * Life in general

5. When do you have difficulty saying no to requests for your time and energy? How do you feel when you say no?

6. How do you handle conflict and confrontation? For example, do you avoid necessary conflict, or pretend conflict isn't happening when it is? Or do you lie and tell yourself that you aren't feeling

certain emotions (e.g., anger, disappointment, confusion) when you actually are? What successes have you had in the past in handling conflicts / confrontations?

7. What was your first reaction when you read that Jesus wasn't always nice?

8. Which upcoming chapters sound the most intriguing to you?

9. What obstacles are most likely to prevent you from finishing this book (e.g., demands of work or home, interruptions, discomfort with new ideas, etc.)? What could you do to set yourself up for success in finishing this book and the study questions?

Bonus Bible Study Question: Read Ezekiel 13:10–12; Malachi 2:6; Matthew 5:9; James 3:17–18; and 1 Peter 3:10–12. From these passages, what do you learn about the differences between peacemakers and peace-fakers?

CHAPTER ONE

The One-Sided Jesus:
Sanctified Sweetness

If you ever went to Sunday school as a child, chances are you saw colorful illustrations of Jesus in action. Remember those? Healing the lame, feeding the five thousand—tremendous miracles performed by a white-robed Jesus with beautiful long brown hair.* He always looked clean, safe, and . . . well . . . nice. Like someone you could bring home to your mother.

*Just how did Jesus keep his hair looking so silky in that arid climate? Now, that was a miracle!

Or perhaps, later in life, you were introduced to this one-dimensional Jesus Christ through sermons or books that presented only the sweet side of Jesus. Go into most churches, and you'll rarely hear a sermon about the firm, confrontational, and courageous side of Jesus' personality. Churches sing about "The Old Rugged Cross," but preachers and teachers seldom mention the rugged side of the Savior. For many women, this is not a problem because . . . let's be honest . . . the rougher side of Jesus can make women uncomfortable and even lead to an occasional cringe.

Gentle Jesus, Meek and Mild?

For example, weren't you just a little taken aback when you learned that Jesus overturned the money changers' tables and whirled a whip around in the temple courts (John 2)? Somebody could have been killed or accidentally gotten an eye put out. At the very least, Jesus made a big mess, and it doesn't say anywhere in Scripture that he helped clean up.

Or what about in Matthew 15 when the Canaanite mother begs Jesus to heal her daughter, and he responds with, "It is not right to take the children's bread and toss it to their dogs" (v. 26). If he were anyone else, believers would denounce him as being hardhearted, cruel, and perhaps not even a Christian because he wasn't polite or helpful. In fact, Jesus sounds rude, like he's calling her a dog. What's up with that?

Far too often, when women come to these passages in the Bible, they just skip over them or try to explain away the stronger side of Jesus. They rationalize, "Jesus wasn't really angry in the temple courts. No way. He was calm and amazingly detached as he swung that whip around." They read in the NIV Bible translation that Jesus rebuked Peter with a stern "Get behind me, Satan! You are a stumbling block to me" (Matthew 16:23), and somehow their NGB (Nice Girl Bible) translation turns that into "Jesus got a little annoyed with Peter and tactfully suggested that it would be best for Peter to give him some space to regroup and have a little 'me time.' "

When Jesus turned water into wine as his first miracle, he made enough vino to fill six huge water vats—over a hundred gallons of wine, more than any wedding party could consume. If anyone else did this, eyebrows would be raised at a show-off who seemed to encourage drunkenness. But it's Jesus, and so believers skim past it.

When Jesus casts out devils, why would a nice savior cast them into a herd of pigs, destroying two thousand animals and what was most likely a family's life savings (Mark 5:13)? He makes no offer to compensate the pigs' owners either. In Matthew 8:18, when surrounded by a crowd of sick people needing healing, Jesus ordered his disciples to take him away to the other side of the lake. That doesn't sound very supportive or compassionate.

At one time he told his disciples to sell their cloaks and buy swords if they did not already have them in order to fulfill the Scripture that "he was counted as one of the bad people" (Luke 22:37 WENT), a fact that has never sat well with his followers, so it's explained away or simply ignored.

Jesus called a nation's religious leaders "whitewashed tombs, which look beautiful on the outside but on the inside are full of dead men's bones and everything unclean" (Matthew 23:27). He declared that he did not come to bring peace "but a sword" (Matthew 10:34), and that he came to "bring fire on the earth" (Luke 12:49).

Though Jesus was not a model of compliance or "good behavior," often women try to put a positive, nonthreatening spin on everything he did, acting like public relations spokeswomen covering for a bungling political candidate. They end up doing damage control for the Son of God—and damaging themselves in the process.

Fortunately, Jesus Christ doesn't need damage control or help from an image consultant. As presented in the Gospels, Jesus is most definitely *not* one-sided. He is the complete embodiment of healthy, balanced human personality; thus, Jesus is immensely compassionate, kind, and gracious while also being assertive, forceful, and firm when necessary. He is good, but he's definitely not "nice" or as safe as many Christians want to believe.

He is a Savior who was fully aware of his actions and words as he lived on earth in human form for thirty-three years. He is also a Savior who says in Matthew 16:24, "If anyone would come after me, he must deny himself and take up his cross and follow me." Not "follow me when I'm nice," but "follow *me*." No qualifiers, just a straightforward command to walk his walk and talk his talk, whether that walk and talk appears nice or not.

What's Wrong With This Picture?

There are several profound problems associated with portraying Jesus as the nicest person to ever skip across ancient soil. First, it's a misrepresentation of Scripture. Presenting half of Jesus (even if it is the gentle half) as the total sum of Jesus requires ignoring almost 20 percent of the verses in the Gospels.[1] That's just wrong. Second Timothy 3:16–17 teaches that *"all* Scripture is God-breathed and is useful for teaching, rebuking, correcting and training in righteousness, so that the man of God may be thoroughly equipped for every good work" (italics added). Every verse about Jesus is in the Bible because God wants it there to develop believers into an accurate image of Christ. And yes, that includes verses where women may wince at the forceful side of Jesus.

Second, a narrow focus on the sweet side of Jesus gives women the idea that God wants Christians to behave sweetly in all situations. Here's the problem: Jesus says in Matthew 5:13, "You are the salt of the earth," not the sugar of the earth. Yes, sugar is delicious, particularly in chocolate desserts. However, salt is infinitely more useful than sugar. Salt enhances natural food flavors, preserves food, and is used in manufacturing over 14,000 products (including glass, rubber, metals, textiles, soap, and cosmetics).[2] Salt, unlike sugar, is necessary for human life.

In Mark 9:50, Jesus says, "Have salt in yourselves, and be at peace with each other," making a clear connection between being like salt and being at peace with others. Your mother may have said, "You can catch more flies with honey than with vinegar," but Jesus wants you to do far more than manipulate people with saccharine pseudo-Christianity. He wants you to be useful in his kingdom and to find following his salty-sweet example practical in everyday life and relationships.* Following the example of an artificially sweet Jesus leads to frustration and has even caused some to walk away from their faith altogether because this example doesn't work well in real life. How could it? It's fake.

Third, portraying Jesus as Mr. Manners in sandals gives the impression that politeness pretty much sums up what it means to be Christlike. The problem here is that hurt people are not drawn toward perfectly nice people. Folks don't look toward women with perfect etiquette for help when life comes crashing down. Hurting people look toward individuals who, like Jesus, have both fire and compassion in their eyes,

*It's no coincidence that most people find a salty-sweet combination of foods irresistible. Snack mix, anyone?

individuals who inspire and who will speak the truth in love—even if it stings. This is the kind of Jesus who attracted "people crowding around him and listening to the word of God" (Luke 5:1), people so numerous that "there was no room left, not even outside the door" (Mark 2:2). If you are going to be a woman who draws people to Christ, you need to reflect to the world an accurate image of Christ, not an image of Miss Manners with a cross around her neck.

A fourth and final serious problem occurs when the Lion of Judah is misrepresented as a precious little lamb: Women lose Christ's complete example of authentic goodness, and over time, begin to sanctify and pursue false niceness instead of true goodness. They substitute something similar for the real thing, guaranteeing disappointing results.

No Substitutions, Please

Have you ever tried to make thick, chewy chocolate chip cookies and ended up with wafer-thin cookies instead? You may have made the error of substituting a margarine spread for butter in the recipe. They look the same and even produce similar-looking dough, but the oven's heat reveals their crucial differences.* True goodness and false niceness are like butter and margarine. They can look similar, but when life's pressures crank up the heat, only authentic goodness will produce the results you want. Far too often, Christian women are fed a watered-down version of Christ's goodness, and consequently believe that timid compliance and superficial sweetness are necessary ingredients for an abundant life. They substitute bland niceness for real goodness, and then when failure results, women blame themselves and believe following Christ's example doesn't work in everyday life. Nothing could be farther from the truth.

*That's assuming you didn't eat all of the raw cookie dough first. Margarine spreads are usually 25 to 50 percent water, so cookie dough made with them will spread more when baked.

True goodness is immensely useful. If you follow Christ's example of goodness, you will find that Christianity works far better than anything else to produce the abundant life. You just have to make sure that your key ingredient is authentic goodness and not a watered-down substitute.

It's the Real Thing

Are you getting hungry to know more about authentic goodness? Here's an inspiring definition from Easton's 1897 Bible Dictionary:

> Goodness in man is not a mere passive quality, but the deliberate preference of right to wrong, the firm and persistent resistance of all moral evil, and the choosing and following of all moral good.[3]

Tweak that definition for modern-day women: Goodness is active. Goodness deliberately chooses to do the right thing and firmly resists what is wrong. Merely avoiding bad things doesn't make women good.

If you want to choose to do the right thing, you have to first know what is right, and that involves getting the mind of Christ—understanding and valuing things the way God does, having his eyes and ears and heart. Having his mind will enable you to clearly distinguish right from wrong, but be forewarned: You will pay a price. When you start thinking like Christ, you are guaranteed to sometimes make choices that offend and anger other people. The Gospels prove this fact. Jesus chose to value and welcome the unwashed masses: prostitutes, tax collectors, partiers, the woman with a perpetual menstrual flow who was deemed "unclean." Jesus chose to honor the impoverished widow's minuscule two-mite offering over the far larger (but less costly) offerings of the wealthy. These choices confused, offended, and infuriated the Pharisees and religious leaders.

Authentic goodness also involves setting yourself apart for service to God. This means you want to do whatever pleases God, which, like having the mind of Christ, comes with a price. Choosing to please him more than anyone else guarantees that occasionally you will make other people unhappy, including family and friends. Prime example: Jesus, again. One time his mother and brothers interrupted his teaching by sending Jesus a message that they were outside, waiting to speak to him. He didn't comply with their request; instead, he used their request to continue his teaching by indicating that his disciples were his family, as well as adding "whoever does the will of my Father in heaven is my brother and sister and mother" (Matthew 12:50). Scripture doesn't record his mother's reaction, but don't you imagine she was put out with Jesus that day? Those were probably hard words for his family to hear, but they needed a reminder that pleasing and serving God was more important to Jesus than pleasing his mother or anybody else.

Contrast that authentic goodness with the false niceness that Christian women often hold as sacred. Instead of focusing on inward goodness, they focus on outward appearances. The focus becomes what they don't do—swear, use bad manners, smoke, get drunk, show cleavage, etc.—and these avoided behaviors are sanctified and held up as the pinnacle of what God wants from women. Meanwhile, what they do for God—attending church, teaching Sunday school, or tithing—can become a performance designed to impress others or to earn God's love. Women begin to sound a lot like the Pharisees, focusing on the outward while ignoring the condition of their inward hearts.

Sit Up Straight

If you're wondering why you have not seen Christ's sweet and salty sides equally presented in church, well . . . join the club. We have wondered about this as well and have some ideas to share with you, but first we want to acknowledge that there have been times when Christians were too forceful and aggressive. Our goal with this book is not to create Christian Mean Girls who bulldoze people. But after helping struggling believers for years, both of us are convinced that the problem isn't that Christians are too spirited; the problem is the opposite: Believers in general aren't spirited or willful enough! As a result, multitudes are underpowered, burned out, and bored with Christianity.

As a body, the church lacks the life skills necessary to be truly like Christ—assertive but not overbearing. Christian women need to find a balance between passivity and aggressiveness. This starts with finding a backbone so that they can be redemptive forces for good in a world that too often strips people of their dignity and worth. Did your mother ever remind you to "stop slumping over and sit up straight"? This book's message is similar: "Stop slumping over and find your Christian backbone. The world needs you."

Hidden in Plain Sight

Given how much the world desperately needs Christian women who will stand up straight, it's surprising how often the firmer side of Jesus is ignored in churches; however, it's no accident. Some church leaders *and* churchgoers have removed Christ's forceful side in a deliberate attempt to make Christianity more appealing to the average person. While this may make sense in a popularity contest, it's foolishness in a church because it robs Christians of a Savior who has the power to actually save and rescue people. Numerous believers are unaware that they've come to a dangerous inner conclusion: "Jesus is so nice that he won't be able to help me out of the trouble I'm in. He's so nice that, like all nice people, he's going to be shocked by how bad the real me can be." Bland niceness may bring a degree of comfort, but it doesn't bring redemption or help create authentic goodness.

And let's admit that not everyone goes to church to pursue righteousness or to change the world. Sometimes women go to church just to get away from the world. Sadly, the world often scares believers far more than it inspires them to redeem it, so women tend to favor churches that make the Good News appear consistently safe and problem-free. This is one of the reasons why believers call the room where they gather a sanctuary.

While church should be a place where people experience peace and refreshment, it should also be a hospital for broken, hurting people who need strength and courage to get back on their feet. The problem is, often people prefer that church be more of a nursery than a hospital: a place that is *always* soothing and pleasant. God never intended for church to be a "wrapped in lambs' wool" experience, because such a place doesn't help believers grow into the full image of Christ, salty and sweet.

When churches resemble nurseries, they attract people looking for comfortable Christianity, a swaddling spirituality that allows them to remain basically unchanged. According to one human behavior specialist who has administered personality tests to thousands of Christians, about 85 percent of churchgoers have more "passive" than "active" personality types, as compared to 62 percent of the general population.[4] This means that fear and timidity may be holding back many churchgoers because their "disease to please" keeps them enslaved to other people's approval. When churches don't provide courage and strength training by showing a full picture of Jesus, passive Christians don't get the spiritual prescription they need to find their backbones. They become resentful doormats in relationships and rarely take meaningful chances in life, severely limiting their spiritual growth.

And this continually sweet and soft but unbiblical Jesus that is primarily taught appeals to women for another reason: Jesus, meek and mild, gives women a head start in the race of faith. His supposed character (always nurturing and compassionate) leans far more toward a typical woman's strengths than a man's—so women get to claim the title of being more spiritual while at the same time not having to undergo the challenging spiritual transformation of becoming more bold, strong, and courageous! It is no wonder, then, that church today is far more attractive to women than men.

The 360-Degree Mirror

The full Jesus is among the best-kept secrets of the Bible—a secret that will change your life unlike any other piece of vital insight. This book's goal is to let you in on this secret so that you can look at Christ and yourself from all perspectives. Have you ever caught a glimpse of yourself in a full-length mirror and been horrified to see that you were walking around with your skirt tucked into the back of your panty hose?* You didn't see the complete picture until you took the time to look at yourself from all angles. Likewise,

*This has happened to one of us, and you can probably guess who.

many women don't have the complete picture of Jesus or themselves because they look only from one viewpoint—the viewpoint that sees and values only the sweet side.

Put yourself into the infamous 360-degree mirror from the TV show *What Not to Wear*, but instead of focusing on your clothing, ask yourself, "Do I reflect the full personality of Jesus Christ?" The goal when emulating the real Jesus is to become both sweet and salty, both gracious and firm. Those qualities complement each other. They make Christ and you deliciously irresistible to a hungry world.

If you need it, consider this your permission to emulate all 360 degrees of Jesus. Sometimes women wait for their parents, pastor, priest, husband, family, or friends to give them permission to be both gracious and firm. That permission may or may not come from those people (you'll find more information about how to handle these people in later chapters). For right now, just know that the Bible permits—commands, actually—that all believers, male and female, be transformed into the full image of Christ.

This essential insight authorizes you to be both stronger and gentler than you may have ever thought possible or allowable. Sometimes it takes a lot of backbone to be tender. In John 8, Jesus demonstrated this when Pharisees brought him a woman caught in adultery. They planned to frame Jesus by trapping him into speaking against Mosaic law and capital punishment. But Jesus, ever wise as a serpent, defused the potentially explosive standoff with one of the most tender and strong statements recorded in the Gospels: "If any one of you is without sin, let him be the first to throw a stone at her" (John 8:7). Gentle mercy and unyielding strength—delivered in one stunning blow.

Don't miss what this statement cost Jesus. He embarrassed and angered the Pharisees, his main rivals throughout his three years of public ministry. They set a trap for Jesus that backfired and instead ensnared them. Jesus knew that his good deed of gentle mercy would ultimately entrench his enemies even further. But because he had the internal strength to withstand their rejection, he could choose to reveal his tender and merciful side even when doing so was dangerous.

Jesus remains history's most captivating figure, in part because he was a full-spectrum person with an amazing twist. He was compassionate when others were judgmental and even hateful. He was bold and courageous when those around him were cowardly. Surrounded by self-righteous, rigid religious people, Jesus stood out as a rare combination of firm, godly truth expressed freely and authentically. And he was able to be so good because he was both tender *and* firm, compassionate *and* courageous. Women tend to think that these traits cancel each other out when, in reality, they complement each other, like a delicious meal that is both sweet and savory. These character traits reflect God's character and nature, and show what complete, 360-degree people are really like, and how they truly live. Understanding this liberating truth is essential to transforming from a Christian Nice Girl into one of God's Good Women.

You'll get more practical tips for putting these insights into daily practice throughout this book, but now it's time to move on to the next factor that causes women to act like Nice Girls instead of powerful, 360-degree women of faith. Has all this talk of sweet and salty food made you thirsty? Not a problem: In the next chapter you'll find two different kinds of soda pop waiting for you.

CNG Nicole

Slowly closing her copy of *No More Christian Nice Girl*, Nicole sits on her couch, slightly taken aback by the chapter she just finished. *I never realized Jesus wasn't nice all the time. How did I miss his forceful, salty side?*

Her cell phone's vibration interrupts her thoughts. Nicole checks the caller ID and sees that her best friend, Shelley, is calling.

"Hey, Shelley. How are you?"

"I'm feeling great after my Sunday afternoon nap. I was wondering if you wanted to ride with me to the women's Bible study class tonight."

"That would be fun. I didn't get all the lessons done, but I still want to go." Nicole pauses. "Shelley, does Bible study help you?"

"What do you mean—like help me understand the Bible?"

"No, I mean, does studying the Bible help you in everyday life?"

Silence, then Shelley slowly replies, "I guess so. I never really thought about it. I do try to apply what we learn, like the 'love your neighbor' stuff."

"Do you ever get frustrated with that? Like being a loving Christian means you have to let other people walk on you?"

"Well, I don't usually let other people run over me, but sometimes I do feel guilty when I stand up for myself. It doesn't seem very Christian. . . . Nicole, why are you asking all these questions?"

"I don't know . . . I'm reading this book, and it's making me think. Did you know that Jesus wasn't always a nice, gentle guy? I feel silly for saying that, but it's like I'm just now seeing the full picture of Christ, and he's not who I thought he was. Don't get me wrong, I still believe that he is the Son of God and our Savior, and that we're supposed to be transformed into his image. But Jesus had a forceful and firm side. If he knew he was doing God's will, he didn't care if his words or actions made people mad."

Shelley laughs. "Yeah, I heard someone say that if Jesus had been a really nice guy, he would have lived to a ripe old age."

"Yeah, that's what I'm talking about. If he had been super sweet all the time and never offended anybody, then the religious leaders wouldn't have plotted to kill him. You know, his tough side is kind of scary. He's not the safe person I always thought he was. I feel like

I'm now seeing something that has been there the whole time, but I somehow missed it."

"Sort of like how you are famous for asking 'Has anybody seen my sunglasses?' and they are always on top of your head?"

Nicole laughs. "Hey, you're the one who searched for thirty minutes for car keys, and they were in your pocket the whole time!"

"You are never going to let me live that down! Okay, I happen to know where my car keys are right now, so I'll be by in an hour to pick you up. I want to hear more about what you're reading."

Study Questions

1. Prior to reading this chapter, what was your overall image of Jesus? Where did you get that picture of Jesus?

2. When you read a Bible passage that describes the confrontational ("salty") side of Jesus, what is your usual reaction?

3. In the past, when you learned about Jesus, were his salty and sweet sides equally represented? If your answer is no, how has this affected your development as a believer? How has this influenced your relationships?

4. In what situations do you feel pressured to act nice and sweet because you are a Christian?

5. Looking over your life right now, where do you most and least reflect the full 360-degree personality of Jesus?

6. How do passive, people-pleasing, Christian Nice Girl behaviors make Christianity seem impractical or not useful in everyday life?

7. Think back over your last seven days. What percentage of your choices were made to please God and what percentage were made to please other people? What could you do to increase your percentage of God-pleasing choices?

8. When and with whom do you tend to focus more on outward appearances than inward goodness as a Christian?

9. What steps could you take to be more authentic at church or in your study group?

10. What can you do to gain a more complete picture of who Jesus Christ is? How will having a fuller picture of Jesus help you, your family, and your friends?

Bonus Bible Study Question: Read Mark 6:30–52. What salty and sweet characteristics did the 360-degree Jesus display during this one 24-hour period in his life?

CHAPTER TWO

Social and Cultural Pressures:
Sugar and Spice and
How We Learned to Act Nice

Do you remember the New Coke fiasco? Coca-Cola executives believed that consumers would prefer a smoother, sweeter-tasting soft drink because their market research had shown that in blind taste tests, people expressed a preference for sweeter sodas. So in April 1985, New Coke was launched. The Coke-drinking public was outraged, and within three months, the company reintroduced the original formula as Classic Coke.[1] The lesson: If the original design is already sweet enough, then stick with that, or you're going to mess up a good thing.

In this chapter, you will learn how the typical woman, as God created her, is like Classic Coke—already sweet enough. Then you will discover how our society, culture, and some churches pressure women to change into New Coke—a too-sweet impersonation of the "real thing." This Nice Girl pressure not only distorts women but also brings out the worst in them. You may be shocked when you see how the Nice Girl Culture is a Petri dish for cattiness.

Hardwiring Clues

Before looking at how God created most women, a quick caveat: The research findings presented are for the majority of women. Some women's brains are wired more like the typical man's brain, and the reverse is true of men as well. Having "majority wiring" is *not* better or more pleasing to God than "minority wiring." Both types of wiring are valuable and useful to God, whether they are found in women or men.

Although Adam and Eve are not available as test subjects, current research on human brains can provide clues into God's original hardwiring for most men and women. Clues are also found in social science research on newborns since male and female babies' innate characteristics have not yet been strongly influenced and modified by their culture. And lastly, looking at how male/female hormonal differences affect brain functioning and behavior sheds light on how God hardwired each sex.

Look Under the Hood and in the Crib

According to Psalm 139, you are wonderfully made and were knit together by the hand of God, whose knitting pattern included making the typical female brain slightly different from the male brain. Not superior or inferior—just different. Overall, the female brain is divinely designed for *relationships*. For example, MRI and PET scans of human brains reveal that, in comparison to the male brain, the typical woman's brain:

- Has language and emotional response control centers located on both sides of the brain, giving women an advantage in language and empathy skills.[2]

- Has a much thicker corpus callosum (the connective tissue between the left and right cerebral hemispheres), allowing women to more quickly transfer data between the hemispheres, as well as have more access to both sides of the brain. More connections between hemispheres, plus language control centers located on both hemispheres, leads to better communication and expression, particularly of feelings.[3]

- Has a larger deep limbic system. The limbic system sets the emotional tone of the mind, stores highly charged emotional memories (positive and negative), modulates motivation and sexual libido, controls appetite and sleep cycles, promotes bonding, and processes the sense of smell. Because of their larger deep limbic system, women in general are more in touch with and better able to express their feelings, better able to connect and bond with others, and more likely to ask, "What's that awful smell?" This larger system also leaves women more vulnerable to depression and getting stuck in repetitive negative thinking.[4]

Female brains are also divinely designed to function differently from male brains. The female brain is quicker to see, smell, and sense danger, and once alerted to danger, reacts with a verbal response— women call out, wanting to connect with others for help, while the male brain reacts to danger with physical action—men fight or flee.[5] Women's brains process touch and sound as more intense, leaving females with more sensitive senses of touch and hearing. These heightened senses, combined with the greater and earlier interest female babies show in people, faces, and eye contact, help explain why girls become more adept than boys at picking up subtle social cues and nuances, and later develop what is called "women's intuition."[6] Newborn girls also demonstrate the female brain's built-in empathetic response when they react more strongly than newborn boys to the sound of another baby crying (and their stronger reaction is not just due to their greater sensitivity to sound).[7]

Making the Connection

Yes, MRI and PET scans confirm what you probably already suspected: God hardwired the majority of female minds to want, to be good at, and to benefit from connection in relationships. In fact, research shows that good conversation with close friends energizes women, helps them clarify complex feelings, raises their self-esteem, and empowers them to take necessary actions.[8] That's why you feel that urge to pick up the phone or e-mail your girlfriends when happy and sad events happen. You may have a husband or male friend who is great to talk with, but there's just something that women can offer that is different, isn't there?

What women can offer is their uniquely created brain that wants to connect with you on an intimate level. If you haven't experienced this with other women, and instead have mainly experienced cattiness, coldness, and competition, you are not alone. Many women have been deeply hurt by their own gender. Later, you'll read an explanation for why females are sometimes catty, and perhaps this may ease your pain and give you the courage to try again with women friends.

The "Love Hormone"

Ah, hormones. Whether you consider them friends or foes, hormones affect brain functioning and behavior. One particularly handy hormone, oxytocin (also known as the "love hormone"), does the following in men and women:

- Releases during hugging, touching, and after orgasm.
- Increases the desire to be near and connected with other people.

- Makes people feel better about the people around them.
- Helps people feel calmer and more relaxed.

In women specifically, oxytocin:

- Is in greater quantities than in men.
- Causes the uterus to contract during childbirth.
- Triggers milk to let down when breastfeeding.
- Plays an important role in mother-infant bonding.
- Plays a central role in responding to stress. [9]

Take note of the final effect listed for oxytocin. God knew that humans would experience stressful, sometimes dangerous situations that require immediate responses. Men's bodies release oxytocin under stress, but its calming effect is dampened when their bodies also release testosterone and vasopressin. That's why most men when stressed or in danger will experience the "fight or flight" response—they are primed to get aggressive or run away. Similarly, women's bodies release oxytocin when stressed or in danger, but because of their higher baseline levels of oxytocin and estrogen (which regulates oxytocin instead of dampening it like male hormones do), most women experience the "tend and befriend" response—oxytocin primes them to care for and connect with others when stressed.[10] That's why if both husband and wife experience the same stressful event, he is more likely to escape to the garage while she is more likely to call a girlfriend to vent. Women's hormones prompt them to turn to others for support and safety, demonstrating again that God divinely designed the typical woman for relationships.

Introducing New Coke

Biology class is now over, and we hope you can see that God created the typical female brain and hormonal responses to support empathetic, intuitive connections with others. That's God's original design for the majority of women—his Classic Coke—and it leads to most women highly valuing relationships. Connections then become like currency for women. They will go to great lengths to have and keep relationships with others because connections are so intrinsically valuable to them.

Not a problem—until society and culture manipulate the original design, "improve" it, and produce mass quantities of too-sweet New Coke, also known as Nice Girls. How does this happen? Through a process called socialization, which everyone participates in.

For example, have you ever found yourself in this tricky situation? You pass your neighbor pushing her newborn baby in a stroller. You want to compliment the baby, but you can't remember whether your neighbor had a boy or a girl, and let's face it, most newborns don't look male or female. They just look like . . . babies. What do you do next to figure out whether to gush over *his* beefy arms or *her* delicate fingers? That's right, you look for clues, like what the baby is wearing or what kind of toys it has, because in American culture, a male baby typically does not wear pink,* and a female baby does not have a tiny football tucked in her stroller by a hopeful father. You check quickly: no football, but the baby is wearing "could-be-either-one" yellow. Fortunately for you, your neighbor's baby is sporting the ultimate gender identifier: a bow. Rest easy, you figured it out—it's a girl.

*Unless his mother, Jennifer, was perpetually running behind on the laundry and had to occasionally dress him in his older sister's pink sleepers. Hey, there was nothing else clean and I had to get to the grocery! Big sigh . . . yes, I know . . . years of therapy ahead for my son.

Sugar and Spice Isn't Always Nice

The bow, the absence of a toy football—these are all signs that a baby girl is being socialized to fit into society's idea of what it means to be a girl. And since she's a girl, guess what her culture says she is supposedly made of? Snips and snails and puppy dog tails? No, according to the nursery rhyme, little girls are made of sugar and spice and everything nice. That doesn't sound so bad, does it? Certainly sounds better than snips and snails, especially since no one knows exactly what a snip is.

However, at the heart of that nursery rhyme is a deeply ingrained set of behavior expectations for males and females. "Boys will be boys"—mischievous, adventurous, rambunctious—and girls . . . well, girls are expected to be sweet, quiet, helpful, tidy, cooperative, and above all, nice. These are what our culture expects of you, and all women. These expectations may be rooted in the typical woman's innate tendencies toward empathy and connection, but society and culture have taken God's physiological design for the majority of women and distorted it into something that limits and even endangers women.

Yes, society has become more accepting of women in the workforce, academia, sports, and leadership positions, but don't think that the sugar-and-spice expectation has melted away like ice cream on a summer day. It's still there, molding and shaping women into Nice Girls, from the pink cradle to the grave.

Sweet Socialization

The sugar-and-spice expectations start in infancy when baby girls are dressed in ruffles, pastels, and bows while boys are dressed in brighter colors and sports-oriented clothing. Adults treat girl babies more gently than boy babies, even though girl babies are physiologically heartier and stronger.[11] Parents provide dolls to daughters and trucks and sports toys to sons, and reward play behavior that is gender stereotyped.[12] Across the world, girls spend more time doing household chores and helping with child care, while boys spend more time in unsupervised play.[13] It's true that girls may prefer to play "relationally" with toys, and may want to be helpful given their empathetic wiring, but when Christian parents, often unknowingly, send solely the message "girls should be nice and helpful and boys should be active and independent," they are hemming in their children and making it more difficult for girls *and* boys to grow into the full 360-degree image of Christ.

Studies show that teachers reinforce boys for assertiveness, speaking up, and thinking independently while girls are praised for being quiet, calm, and neat.[14] When teachers encourage girls to focus on details and praise them for following rules, the seeds of perfectionism are sown, leading some girls to avoid taking risks because they are afraid of producing imperfect work. Girls who are willing to take risks and be assertive are likely to have their behavior labeled as disruptive and negative.[15]

In children's textbooks and fiction, males are represented far more often than females,[16] and passive females are often rescued by adventurous, competent male figures.[17] Sadly, by the time girls are in sixth and seventh grade, they rate being popular and well-liked as more important qualities than being competent or independent.[18] Even in college, women are not free from the Nice Girl pressure: Research indicates that faculty members tend to take more seriously the classroom discussion contributions made by male students, allow men to dominate discussions, call on men more often, and are more likely to remember male students' names.[19]

The media also fashions girls into the sugar-and-spice pattern, and studies suggest that when various media (television, movies, Internet, music, magazines, video games, etc.) are combined, girls currently consume over seven and a half hours of entertainment media per day.[20] While those media do provide some positive role models of females using their intelligence and acting independently, the overwhelming message sent is that girls and women are more concerned with romance, dating, and appearance, while men focus on their occupations.[21] As Lyn Mikel Brown explains in her book *Girlfighting*, often "movies send the message that there is one *acceptable* avenue to power: be nice . . . look beautiful. . . . Come off too bold, say what you think too loudly, take up too much space, express your anger and disappointment, and you risk casting your lot with the evil ones."[22]

Even "family friendly" media subtly reminds females that Nice Girls stay in the background. One study evaluated the 101 top-grossing G-rated films from 1990 to 2004 and found that 75 percent of the overall characters were male and 83 percent of the narrators were male.[23] Things don't get better as female viewers develop more adult viewing habits: Another study revealed that major network news featured female expert commentators 13 percent of the time and male experts 87 percent of the time.[24] Is anyone out there getting the message that nice women should look pretty and keep their opinions to themselves?

Church Girls Gone Mild

Of course, no book on the Christian Nice Girl problem would be complete without looking at how the church socializes girls and women. Rather than trying to resolve every "hot button" doctrinal issue related to gender, such as whether women should serve as pastors, here's a simple observation that rings true for many female believers: The sugar-and-spice expectations and pressures that women face are often even worse inside than outside the church's walls. Some churches don't allow women to be involved in any form of leadership, unless it's singing on the worship team or teaching children. This means that the important insights and contributions available from women's God-given, intuitive, empathetic minds are undervalued, unheard, and unheeded. In other churches, when women are encouraged to be more assertive and expressive, it's often highly compartmentalized.

Being animated and spirited is okay—but only during worship. It's good to be courageous—when sharing the gospel. It's right to be firm—when disciplining your children.

And when women are allowed to lead, some are trained that when it comes to a disagreement, men win by virtue of gender, not accuracy. I (Paul) experienced this one evening as my wife and I joined three other couples in a quaint courtyard. One of the women and I began debating a theological issue. For about twenty minutes, we were the only ones talking at the table, two people passionately defending their opinions. My wife, Sandy, kicked me numerous times under the table to *let it go.*

But before I could concede that we would have to agree to disagree on the topic (Sandy's pointy shoes really hurt after a while), I was astonished by how the woman ended the debate.

"I disagree, but you're a man, so you're probably right."

"What?" I said, in quiet bewilderment. "That's . . . that's an excuse, not a reason."

I felt sorry for this bright and anxious woman. Just because I'm a man doesn't mean I'm automatically right in discussions. However, that's what her church had socialized her into believing: She was supposed to bow to any man who disagreed with her regarding theological matters, even when she believed that his opinion was dead wrong. She ended up trying to please me instead of remaining true to her understanding of God and his Word.

This is what many women are socialized to do in church: please people, not God. They come to church experiencing ongoing pressure from the world to be plastic Nice Girls, and the church, instead of freeing women to emulate the 360-degree Jesus, influences them to become even more of a smiley-face doormat, by teaching them that this is what God expects from women: quiet, sweet, unrelenting compliance.

But God's purpose in creating the average woman with empathy and connection skills is not to produce perpetually nice, hyper-compliant, non-boat-rocking women—it can't be, since Jesus (as you saw in chapter 1) was not particularly nice or compliant, and he definitely made waves. God wants women to reflect all 360 degrees of Christ's image, which means that truly good Christian women won't look as sweet and unassuming as their church may expect.

A woman who doesn't meet her church's sugar-and-spice expectations will find a frustrating force working against her: the "selective perception" that some church leaders and churchgoers unknowingly practice. They see or hear only the Bible verses or sermons that support what they already believe: that God expects women to be Christian Nice Girls. Scripture or sermons that support female (and male) believers embracing the full sweet-and-salty personality of Jesus simply don't register, even when they are presented.

Girl Interrupted

There's a final powerful social force shaping girls to be sugar and spice: other girls. Sociologists have discovered that as early as elementary school, girls have established in their minds what an ideal female should act and look like. They model their behavior accordingly and then bestow popularity on girls who most closely match this imaginary paragon of womanhood. Now, who do you think their idealized female is more like—Condoleezza Rice or Paris Hilton? It's not the former Secretary of State. Research indicates that even young girls know that their status comes from physical attractiveness, clothing, social skills, romantic success with boys, their parents' higher socioeconomic status (and the resulting expensive clothing, material possessions, and lifestyle), their parents' permissive parenting style (less parental supervision means more freedom), and (last on the list, sadly) academic performance.[25] Girls, having been socialized previously by adults to be compliant and over-focused on outward appearances, socialize other girls in turn, and create a culture of "compliance and conformity," wherein girls closely follow social roles and rules, and enforce them on other girls.[26]

In a nutshell, countless studies have shown that gender socialization gives girls "roots," and boys "wings," meaning that girls are shaped by their culture to become interdependent while boys are shaped for autonomy and independence. Being interdependent or connected through relationships is not a bad thing. The problem arises when that's your only option, when independence, assertiveness, and speaking the truth are not options. Take those out of the mix, and you've got a sure-fire recipe for cattiness.

How the Nice Girl Culture Breeds Cattiness

"Catty, that's just how girls are. You can't trust them," says fifteen-year-old Amber, sitting rigidly with her fists clenched as she relays the painful story of her former best friend's betrayal. "She said she didn't like my boyfriend, but then people told me she made out with him at a party. Then she started telling people that he wanted to dump me because *I* was a slut!" Amber's anger suddenly dissolves into tears of hurt. "She's been my best friend since second grade! How could she do this to me?"

Amber's all-too-familiar story illustrates the relational aggression (spreading rumors about someone, teasing, threatening to exclude someone, shunning) that girls commit against one another. Girls use these behaviors primarily to bully other girls.[27] Physical punches may not be thrown, but the emotional pain is devastating and, over time, can lead girls and women to believe that females, by nature, are untrustworthy, devious, and manipulative—in a word, catty. But is this really true? Are females born catty?

Girls *learn* cattiness from sitting at the knee of the Nice Girl culture, in and outside of church. You've already seen that God's original design was to hardwire most women for empathy, intuition, and connectedness. He gave them greater skills with language and emotions. Physiologically speaking, the majority of women are primed to highly value relationships and find disconnection from others very painful. Then women are socialized from infancy to believe that if they want to keep their relationships, they must behave like Nice Girls: unrelentingly helpful, pleasant, quiet, self-effacing, noncompetitive, and compliant—no matter the situation.

As they move into the upper grades of elementary school, they also experience increasingly unrealistic cultural expectations for beauty, as well as behavior. This is a lot of pressure on nine- and ten-year-olds, and it makes them anxious because who can match up to these ridiculous standards? Answer: no one. But that's not what magazines and television and, yes, sometimes even parents and the church tell them, and so girls begin to experience shame over their inability to meet impossible cultural standards that are actually cruel to all but a chosen few.[28] And shame, anxiety, and jealousy give birth to cattiness. Lyn Mikel Brown explains,

> *Girls take out their anxieties and fears about matching up to or resisting ideals of feminine beauty and behavior on each other. They fight—exclude, tease, reject, and torment—other girls over things the dominant culture makes out to be very important, but in the grand scheme of things shouldn't matter that much—that is, how perfectly nice, thin, or pleasing a girl is.*[29]

Adding to their shame and fear of not measuring up, girls learn from their culture that anger, open and expressed, is forbidden for Nice Girls. Christian Nice Girls get the double whammy: Anger is not just wrong for women, it's sinful. From all directions, girls learn *"Don't speak up, don't speak the truth, don't get angry, preserve your relationships at all costs,"* so they learn to avoid confrontation and use hidden ways of getting what they want. Tragically, by not being honest and straightforward with others as Christ modeled, Christian girls sabotage the very relationships they are trying to preserve. (We'll discuss this further in chapters 5 to 7.)

Because they are human, girls do get angry. They fight, disagree, and compete, but since they've learned that adults disapprove of girls expressing these feelings, they take their angry feelings underground or out of the sight of adults.

Brown adds,

> Girls learn early to use covert tactics like threatening to damage or control a girl's relationships with others or to ignore or exclude someone they are angry with. . . . The ultimate threat when a young girl feels the wrath of another girl is not being yelled at or hit, but excluded: "You can't come to my birthday party." In this way, adults' expectations that girls be nice and cooperative and avoid loud conflicts . . . set the stage for a more opaque, but no less aggressive, form of girlfighting.[30]

And so the Nice Girl Culture, instead of producing girls who are honest, kind, strong, brave—the kind of truly good women who can change the world—actually produces the opposite: catty girls who believe their only option is to use relational aggression to both get what they want and to protect themselves from the shame of not measuring up to their culture's unrealistic standards. Girls learn to lie to each other, not because females are born untrustworthy or devious, but because it just seems too risky to speak the truth. Sow this poisonous seed over a lifetime and you will reap, as many Christian Nice Girls do, a harvest of superficial, unsatisfying relationships—relationships where "everybody signs their letters with love or dots their I's with hearts—even when they don't feel like it."[31]

So there you have it. A Tale of Two Sodas: Will you choose to give in to the unrelenting cultural pressure to be too-sweet New Coke with its inevitable cattiness? Or will you courageously choose to be Classic Coke and be plenty sweet enough, just as God originally created you? It's your choice.

CNG Nicole

"Mom, guess what?" Heather swings her backpack up onto the kitchen table. "After track practice, Coach Collins asked me to consider being the team captain."

"Honey, that's wonderful!"

Heather grabs an apple and talks around mouthfuls. "Yeah, I thought he would ask Jonathan. Do you think I should say yes?"

"Do you want to be team captain?"

"I think so, but Jonathan might get mad at me because he wasn't picked. Some guys don't like girls who are leaders."

"Heather, are you sweet on Jonathan?"

"Mom! I didn't say I liked him! Anyway, a bunch of other girls like him."

Nicole smiles at her daughter. "It's okay for you to like him too. But if he gets mad because you're the team captain, then he's not worthy to be your boyfriend."

Heather pauses, apple raised halfway to her mouth. "I can't believe you just said that. You sound like Dad. He's usually the one telling me stuff like that."

"What do I usually tell you?"

Putting one hand on her hip, Heather furrows her brow and says in an exaggeratedly high voice, "Now, Heather, don't be bossy. You don't always have to voice your opinion, young lady."

Nicole winces at the all-too-accurate imitation. "Okay, I may have gone overboard trying to get you to not make waves. You are a natural-born leader, honey. That can scare me because I've experienced firsthand how hard people can be on girls who speak their mind."

Heather settles into a chair, looking interested. "Really? What happened?"

Nicole slices vegetables as she explains. "Back in high school, I noticed that the girls' sports teams didn't get the same access to the workout gym as the guys' teams did, and they also didn't get as much publicity as the guys did. But according to Title IX, the girls' and guys' sports are supposed to be equal. So I wrote a school newspaper article about the unfair situation, and when it came out, the principal and coaches were really mad. They told me I didn't know what I was talking about."

"That's terrible! Grandma and Grandpa should've had them fired!"

Nicole laughs ruefully. "No, your grandparents weren't too happy with me either, particularly when I told them I got called to the principal's office over the article. At the time, I couldn't handle everyone being angry with me. I felt all alone. Maybe that's when I started believing it was better to keep my mouth shut than to risk upsetting other people. I hope you won't make that same mistake. Anyway, if you believe God wants you to be the track team captain, then go for it. If Jonathan gets mad, then he's not the one for you."

"Okay, I'll think about it." Heather heads for the kitchen door, then turns toward her mother. "Thanks for telling me your story. I'm sorry that everyone got mad at you."

Nicole cocks an eyebrow at Heather. "Well, it turned out that not *everyone* was mad. Your dad said reading that article made him decide to ask me out. He thought I showed spunk. I guess he had figured out that life can be tough for girls."

"Yeah, it can be tough, but I'm glad I'm a girl. We have cuter shoes."

Nicole laughs. "Yes, we do. It is good to be a girl."

Study Questions

1. God created male and female brains and hormones with similarities and differences. Which of the differences are most intriguing or surprising to you? Why do you think God created these differences?

2. What kinds of situations make you want to connect with other people?

3. Think back to your childhood. What were society's expectations for boys vs. girls at school, home, church, and in the media? Have those expectations changed now?

4. Have you experienced "sugar and spice" expectations to be perpetually nice, compliant, quiet, and helpful in a church setting? If yes, how has this affected you spiritually?

5. Do you prefer male or female friends? Why?

6. Have you experienced cattiness (relational aggression from other females)? If so, how did this affect you? How did it affect your opinion of females?

7. What can you do to help a girl who is experiencing cattiness, being catty herself, or feeling pressure from the Nice Girl Culture?

8. What Nice Girl Culture expectations are frustrating to you? What could you do in response to those unrealistic expectations?

Bonus Bible Study Question: Read 1 Samuel 16:7; Proverbs 11:22; 31:30; Jeremiah 17:10; John 7:24; and 2 Corinthians 5:9–12. According to these passages, how does God evaluate you and how does this differ from the way the world evaluates you?

CHAPTER THREE

Harmful Childhood Experiences: Sifted Sugar

Since the chocolate chip cookies from chapter 1 have mysteriously disappeared, how about joining us in the kitchen so we can make a loaf of warm, delicious-smelling banana bread?* Grab an old-fashioned sifter so you can mix together the dry ingredients. Watch closely as you turn the crank, crushing lumps into fine powder. Such a useful process if you are making quick breads—such a painful process if you are the lump and life's difficult experiences are grinding away at you and influencing you to act like a Nice Girl instead of a powerful, 360-degree woman of faith.

*We never said reading this book would help you stay on your diet.

Many Christian Nice Girls who were emotionally sifted during childhood want to believe that these painful events are safely in the past, never to bother them again; however, we have seen during years of working with hurting people that the aftereffects of certain harmful childhood experiences often intensify current problems with passivity, people pleasing, and fear-based decision making. When CNGs avoid the often difficult but necessary look into their childhood influences, they sentence themselves to very small lives, full of internal and external conflicts. Instead of learning how to do conflict well, they avoid it at all costs, setting themselves up for even more painful experiences with manipulative people.

God Allows Sifting

God understands that painful sifting is a part of human life. He allowed Satan to afflict Job with devastating personal, financial, and physical loss. Jesus told Simon Peter at the Last Supper that Satan had asked to sift him as wheat. God loved these men, and yet he still allowed their agonizing siftings. As hard as it is to understand why God allows bad things to happen to adults like Job and Peter, it's even harder to comprehend his purpose behind the bad things that happen to children. We aren't trained seminarians who can give you a beautifully written theological explanation of pain's divine purpose. This aside, we would like to explain how three particular types of difficult experiences sift women and can leave them vulnerable to hiding their authentic selves behind a brittle façade of fake smiles. Those girlhood experiences are:

1. Lacking inspiring role models and encouraging words.
2. Having anxious, overprotective parents.
3. Enduring emotional, physical, or sexual abuse.

You may have encountered one or all of these negative experiences, which fall along a continuum from less intense to very intense. For example, some women have experienced occasional verbal abuse while others have experienced horrendous physical or sexual abuse. Christian Nice Girls tend to minimize their negative experiences by saying, "What happened to me wasn't that bad. Other people have had it worse." Yes, perhaps other people have had it worse, but that doesn't mean that what happened to you should be ignored or judged as unworthy of examination. You have to look for what's perpetuating a problem before you can fix it.

Coconut or Peach?

Christian Nice Girls also beat themselves up for struggling with losses and trauma. If you find yourself asking, "Why am I always the one struggling? My siblings/other people went through what I went through, and they seem to be doing just fine," please know that:

- People who look like they are doing fine aren't always doing fine underneath.

- Some people are blessed with resilient nervous systems and temperaments. Things just roll off their backs more easily. They are emotionally built like coconuts—harder to bruise. Other people are blessed with more sensitive nervous systems and temperaments. They are often empathetic, imaginative people who sense everything (changes, emotions, smells, textures, etc.) more intensely. They are emotionally built like peaches—easier to bruise. If God made you a peach, you will likely struggle more to heal from difficult experiences than a coconut will.

- Having multiple early losses and traumas that weren't adequately addressed at the time they happened can affect your brain development and make your nervous system more easily overwhelmed by emotions later in life. Experiencing repeated trauma early in life can even turn a coconut into a peach.[1] However, practicing assertiveness and other healthy behaviors can strengthen your ability to "take it all in stride."

As you read this chapter, try to take a clear-eyed look at the parenting you received without condemning your parents for their mistakes. Many parents are not fully aware of their behavior's harmful effects. Often, the damage was not done out of malice, but out of ignorance. This in no way excuses deliberate abuse where the harm is glaringly obvious and cruelly disregarded or denied by parents or other perpetrators.

Looking for a Few Good Women

Let's start by looking at how lacking inspiring role models and encouraging words sifts girls and leaves them vulnerable as adult women to the Christian Nice Girl problem. When you were growing up, who were your female role models? Perhaps you admired a relative, a teacher, or a friend's mother. I (Jennifer) will admit to admiring . . . this is so embarrassing . . . Wonder Woman. More specifically, Lynda Carter in the TV role of Wonder Woman. Her flawlessly coiffed hair and stunning blue eyes perfectly complemented her gold boots. Somehow she could run up a rocky hillside in those high-heeled boots with nary a slip or slide. Plus, she didn't need a male superhero to come in and rescue her. Nope, she could take care of the bad guys herself using her golden lariat and bullet-deflecting cuffs. She was beautiful, but she was also strong.

Little girls need gracious, strong women in their lives so they can learn firsthand how to be both feminine and firm. These role model women don't have to be as beautiful as Wonder Woman to take your breath away. Instead, their inspiring courage and boldness encourage others to shoot for the stars. When I was in high school, my mom went back to college to get her teaching degree. She would be the first person in my family to graduate from college, and she did it while raising three teenagers. From her example, I learned that anything was possible for me, no matter how daunting my circumstances.

Not every girl is blessed with that kind of female role model who blazes a trail that gives others hope that they too can follow the same path. When you grow up lacking assertive female role models, you don't have any footsteps to follow in. You have to blaze your own trails, and swinging a machete through the tangle of confusing messages and expectations from the Nice Girl Culture is frustrating, spirit-draining work when girls don't have confident, strong women to go behind. Sometimes it just seems easier to tag along with the passive role models who have trudged down a deceptively smooth trail of over-compliance, conflict avoidance, and people pleasing. Whose footsteps are you following? Do you like where they are taking you?

Listening for a Few Good Words

Also think about the messages you heard about what is and is not acceptable behavior for you or females in general. Words powerfully shape children. Did you hear encouraging words like this?

- "You can do it, I believe in you."
- "It's okay to make a mistake. Better to have tried and failed than to not have tried at all."
- "You can do anything you set your mind to."
- "Great job!"
- "God has blessed you with a smart brain. Try that advanced math class."
- "Wow, you really put forth great effort."
- "You've got a natural talent for this."
- "Who cares what other people think? Just be yourself."
- "If you work hard, you can make it happen."
- "You have a much better chance of getting what you need and want if you ask for it directly. So just ask."
- "Everyone gets afraid sometimes, but don't let your fear stop you from doing the right thing."
- "Whatever God has planned for you, he will equip you to do."

Or did you hear discouraging words like this?

- "Why do you want to try something stupid like that? You can't do that."
- "You are just going to embarrass yourself/the family if you try to do that."
- "Look who is getting too big for her britches!"
- "You missed a spot—again. Why can't you do anything right?"
- "Men aren't attracted to brainy women. You better dumb down if you want a boyfriend."
- "You won't follow through, so don't even start."
- "You just aren't any good at this."
- "What will the neighbors think?"
- "That's a pipe dream. Give it up."
- "Stop being so forward. Just keep your hand down and your mouth shut."
- "Don't make waves. Just act nice."
- "God doesn't like little girls who act like that."

Now imagine the cumulative impact of these words spoken to a woman over her lifetime. If she hears the first list of inspiring words, she's going to believe in herself and in God's love and providence. She's going to take some risks and live big. She, like everyone, will occasionally stumble or fail, but she has the emotional resources and faith in God to pick herself up and try again.

If she hears the second list of discouraging words, she's going to doubt herself and God's love for her. She will live small, avoiding even the smallest risks. When opportunities come her way, she will wait anxiously for the proverbial other shoe to drop instead of resting confidently in God's provision for her. She will think that the world is a dangerous place filled with people who can't be trusted. She'll be easily discouraged and influenced.

When I (Jennifer) was a high school senior, my biology teacher, Denny Lester, told me about a new scholarship program at his alma mater, Transylvania University,* a private college whose tuition my family could not afford. When I talked to my school counselor (we'll call him Mr. Smith) about applying for the scholarship, he said, "You can't get that scholarship. Your scores aren't good enough. Don't waste your time applying." Now, you have to understand something. This was the first time in my life that I had ever heard someone tell me that I shouldn't even try. Had I grown up hearing discouraging words from the second list, I would have believed Mr. Smith and slunk away to my next class, hopes dashed and spirits sunk.

*No vampire jokes, please. Transylvania University, located in Lexington, Kentucky, is the oldest liberal arts college west of the Allegheny Mountains.

However, because I was blessed with a childhood full of encouraging words from the first list, plus I had inspiring female role models (remember my mom, who was in college at this point?), Mr. Smith's discouraging words did not defeat me.

No, his words made me angry, which was good, because that helped push me past my fear of offending Mr. Smith. I could sense he would be displeased if I did apply because, as my counselor, he was required to "waste" his time writing my recommendation letter. I took a deep breath, summoned my courage, and said, "I'm going to apply anyway." And then I bolted from his office before he could talk me out of applying, feeling both panicky and proud that I had stood up for myself.

What happened? God blessed me with that scholarship.* And going to college led to going to graduate school and getting my doctorate. Turns out a scholarship can take you more places than Wonder Woman's gold boots ever could.

*A thousand thanks to Mr. Lester for believing in me.

Give Yourself What You Weren't Given

If you lacked role models and encouraging words, you can learn to give yourself what you weren't given. Look around your church, neighborhood, and workplace for women who are known for being strong but also gracious. Study them and how they react to situations. Listen to what they say and how they say it. Get to know them if you can. When the time is right, ask one of them if you can get together for coffee.

Be careful how you interpret her response to you. Christian Nice Girls, because they fear rejection, tend to get their feelings hurt when other people have good boundaries and say things like, "I'm busy right now. Let's look at next month." Also, look for women who actually have room in their lives for an occasional lunch with you. If they are working outside the home while raising children, they simply may not have any extra time for you during this season of their life. Don't despair—God has other wonderful women in mind for you. Keep looking, and remember that you can learn a lot by observing a role model woman, even if you don't have an intimate relationship with her. For example, in the next chapter, you'll meet God's Good Women from Bible times and modern history, and you'll acquire numerous helpful lessons from studying their lives.

In addition, you can give yourself the encouraging words you desperately need to hear. Photocopy the first list, tape it to your mirror, and read it to yourself every morning and before bed. Add Scriptures and other statements that inspire and challenge you. Reach out to your friends and ask them for "booster shots" of encouragement when you need them. Whenever I (Jennifer) got discouraged while writing this book, I sent e-mails letting my friends know that I was struggling and needed prayers. Within a day, my inbox would be filled with encouraging words.

Don't hesitate to ask for what you need. Most people feel blessed by the opportunity to support someone else as they previously have been supported. As 2 Corinthians 1:3–4 says,

> *Praise be to the God and Father of our Lord Jesus Christ, the Father of compassion and the God of all comfort, who comforts us in all our troubles, so that we can comfort those in any trouble with the comfort we ourselves have received from God.*

Anxious and Overprotective Parents

Let's move on to the second difficult childhood experience that predisposes girls to develop the Christian Nice Girl problem: having anxious, overprotective parents. You inherited your eye color and perhaps your oddly shaped toes from Mom and Dad, but did you know that your parents also can also transmit their view of the world to you? Not directly through their genes, but through countless interactions and choices, your parents let you know how they see the world and life in general. For Christian Nice Girls with anxious parents, the message transmitted was *"Life is to be feared."*

This type of caretaker hovers like a search-and-rescue helicopter, transmitting fear and overprotecting children by:

- Not allowing them to regularly go outside and play in a reasonably safe neighborhood, but watching them like a hawk when they are allowed outside, which thwarts their play.
- Setting limits that would only be appropriate for a much younger child on how far they can ride their bikes or walk with friends.
- Overreacting to and overanalyzing normal childhood developmental challenges or minor injuries.
- Painting a verbally frightening picture of the world by continually pointing out any possible dangers, however remote or unlikely.

- Performing tasks that they could do themselves (like cutting older children's meat during meals), which reinforces beliefs of inferiority and powerlessness.

- Intruding into and trying to control all aspects of their children's free time, relationships, and jobs.

- Constantly calling them on their cell phone (an electronic umbilical cord) just to "see how they're doing."

- Making all of their children's decisions.

- Rescuing their children from any mistakes and not allowing them to suffer any negative consequences.

Instead of keeping children safe, fearful over-parenting makes children timid and fragile—the kind of children that adult predators prey on and that bullies target. With the best of intentions, parents who shield their children from all of life's difficulties actually make their children's lives harder, especially as they become adults. Such children are growing older but not growing up.

Parents perform these overprotective behaviors in the name of love, but look closely and you'll see that they are actually motivated by fear. And making choices out of fear leads to short-range, selfish decision making: Parents choose whatever makes them feel immediately less anxious instead of looking at what is best for their children in the long run.

For example, when overprotective parents are afraid of the necessary pain that comes from watching their daughter make normal mistakes, and choose to "protect" her by making all her decisions, she won't ever learn how to make independent decisions. Instead, she will wait for others to tell her what to do, perhaps because the decision-making part of her brain never fully developed. Over the long run, this sets her up to be passively subservient in relationships. She will easily yield to powerful peers and be prime pickings for manipulative men who want to control or sexually exploit her.

Likewise, when overprotective parents rescue a daughter from the consequences of any mistakes she might be allowed to make, she doesn't get to learn crucial life lessons that are best taught by the real world. She won't know what adversity feels like or how to handle it, so when hard times come in adulthood, she's a deer caught in the headlights—overwhelmed and paralyzed by fear. She may become a perfectionist, unrealistically hoping that doing things perfectly will calm her anxious heart and keep her safe.

Simply by watching fearful parents worry about what might happen, girls can learn to invent things to fear, and will then live small in the scary imaginary Land of What If. They play it safe, even when that means falling behind their peers and missing out on opportunities and dreams.

Moving Past Fear

While you can't prevent inheriting your oddly shaped toes (truly, they are part of your charm), you can learn to overcome any unreasonable fears that anxious, overprotective parents may have passed down to you. First, recognize where cowardice is rearing its ugly head in your life. Women don't usually think of cowardice as a particularly bad thing because the Nice Girl Culture allows females to get away with timidity. But when women shrink back from doing the right thing because they fear potential pain or loss, it's called—gulp—cowardice.

And God takes the sin of cowardice very seriously. Revelation 21:8 states, "The cowardly, the unbelieving, the vile, the murderers, the sexually immoral, those who practice magic arts, the idolaters and all liars—their place will be in the fiery lake of burning sulfur." Cowardice is included among the worst temptations you can give in to.

Cowardice can be difficult to spot because a cowardly spirit and a gentle spirit can appear outwardly similar, but look inward, and your real motives will reveal the difference. So ask yourself: "Am I holding back here (not saying or doing something) because doing so is the wise, loving choice, or because I'm fearful of what I might lose (popularity, money) or what I might gain (negative attention, criticism, retaliation)?"

It's also helpful to ask yourself if your fear is reality-based or merely False Evidence Appearing Real (FEAR). Many fears are counterfeit. They seem frighteningly real, but look closer, and you'll see that what you are afraid of is often something that is highly unlikely to happen. Don't let something that isn't even real scare you into the very real sin of cowardice.

Second, you can learn much about moving past the fears passed down to you by talking with courageous people. Courage is far more caught than taught, so seek out the company of the courageous. Study them and ask them questions about how they pushed past their fears. And don't overlook people from history, including Jesus. He faced every fear imaginable, so spend time with the real Jesus. When you rub shoulders with someone, you take on their characteristics, and there's no one better to resemble than the 360-degree Jesus. As you study the Bible, make notes in a journal each time you read how Jesus faced an anxiety-inducing situation and chose to do what was right, not what was easy or safe. Each time you see Jesus facing fear, give yourself permission to be like him.

Third, take small steps toward facing your fears so that you build your courage to eventually face them head-on. For example, if you're afraid to make financial decisions, such as buying a house or investing in stocks/bonds, begin with a small step, like making an appointment with a real estate agent or financial planner. You will likely feel a strong pull to let the professionals make all the decisions for you— fight this urge because you need to develop your discernment and decision-making skills.

Fourth, remember that your body can be your friend when it

comes to facing fears and growing courage. When anxious, breathe deeply from your stomach. Within three to four deep breaths, you will feel less afraid and more clearheaded. Also, put a slight smile on your face. Yes, that sounds weird, but doing so will make you feel less fearful inside and look more confident to others. Fatigue can make a coward of anyone, so if your body is tired, irrational fears can appear alarmingly real. Get more rest, and you'll likely find facing fear easier.

Lastly, if you are a parent trying to move past the fears handed down to you, examine how you relate to your own children. Are you unknowingly passing on the same *"Life is to be feared"* message that you heard? If so, push past your fear of the unknown, and allow your children age-appropriate freedoms and the blessing of learning from their mistakes. Scary "what-ifs" may crowd your mind, but don't let them control your parenting. Breathe deeply, turn your worry list into your prayer list, and talk to a counselor if your anxiety interferes with daily living.

An Upside-Down World

Encountering abuse is the final difficult experience that sifts girls and leaves them vulnerable to becoming Christian Nice Girls as adults. Whether it's verbal, emotional, physical, spiritual, or sexual, abuse deeply shames its victims and leaves them believing lies, such as:

- "I deserved what happened to me. It was my fault."
- "I am worthless/stupid/bad/dirty/unwanted."
- "I am forever flawed."
- "I need to hide because no one would like the real me."
- "If people knew what happened to me, they would reject me."
- "What happened wasn't that bad/wasn't really abuse."

- "Other people are always smarter and better than me."
- "I'm a constant screw-up."
- "I'll never be good at anything."
- "God doesn't love me."

If you experienced abuse, you know what it's like to live in a dangerous, unpredictable world where everything is upside down. Healthy actions are condemned, normal needs are shamed, speaking the truth is punished, and exerting your will can be deadly; while unhealthy actions are the only way to survive: Hide your thoughts, numb your feelings, give in quickly, deny the painful truth, keep unwanted secrets. Surviving abuse, as a child or an adult, often means that you have to play by your abuser's rules—rules that set you up to behave like a fearful, passive person long after you have escaped the abuse.

I (Paul) experienced the upside-down, confusing world of childhood abuse. I walked on eggshells as a kid because one moment my mother was warm and nurturing, and within minutes it was like a switch was thrown deep within her, and she would turn angry, abusive, and disdainful. I was thrown across the room by my hair, slapped, punched, kicked, and hit with household items like brooms and vacuum cleaner attachments.

But it's the verbal and emotional abuse that lingered long after my physical wounds healed. My mother told me I was worthless, stupid, and even evil for committing common childhood blunders. Her use of sarcasm was especially cutting. When my elementary school administrators informed her that my test scores indicated that I was bright, and asked for her permission to place me in the gifted program, I heard her bitter laugh and caustic reply: "Him? He can't even find his shoes in the morning."

Most parents lose it occasionally, say or do things that they regret, and later apologize. My experience was beyond this. I cannot remember my mother ever apologizing for her cruel and contemptuous behavior, which was intended to strip me of my God-given dignity. Her abuse was designed to pierce my core and steal my self-worth. She succeeded. It has taken courage to confront the lies that come with abuse, and years of personal soul work to understand what really happened and heal from it.

My home was a dangerous place, so it was only natural that I would feel tremendous fear there. But, like many abuse survivors, I generalized this fear to include the entire world. I began to believe the lie that all people and experiences are dangerous, a lie that produces two fear-based extreme responses: overreacting or underreacting.

The Hidden Cost of Underreacting

Overreacting happens when fearful people try to protect themselves by adopting an aggressive "I'll get you before you get me" attitude. Guarded and defensive, they overreact when no harm was even intended. They come across as irritable and prickly, but there is a frightened person under all that bluster.

In contrast, instead of overreacting to words or behaviors that might threaten their well-being, fearful CNGs *underreact*. They respond passively to life because that is what they had to do to survive their upbringing. When parents explode unpredictably, children survive by learning *"Don't make waves or things will get even worse."* The problem is, when you won't make necessary waves as an adult, you end up drowning in a sea of timidity and mediocrity. You will sink into an ultrasafe, but ultimately unsatisfying life marked by resentment when others, who are willing to take risks, swim past you.

When children are called names or beaten, they survive by learning *"Don't fight back or things will get even worse."* Then, as adults, they find themselves accepting poor treatment and are petrified by needed confrontations. They felt devalued early in life by cruel words and actions, and later they won't defend themselves because they mistakenly believe they have no value.

When children are emotionally neglected and left to fend for themselves, they survive by learning *"Don't even try, because it will only make things worse."* Then they go into adulthood living small, passive lives, hoping to remain unnoticed because they falsely believe that they are hopelessly inadequate.

When children are shamed for expressing normal needs, valid emotions, or personal opinions, they survive by learning *"Deny your needs, ignore your feelings, and don't have an opinion, or things will get even worse."* As adults, they then discover that they have lost touch with their core—they don't know what they feel, need, or truly believe.

What helped Christian Nice Girls survive abuse—under-reacting—now costs them dearly as adults. Ultimately, underreacting to life out of fear costs the most precious thing you have to offer: yourself.

The Abuse Wasn't Your Fault

If you are a Christian Nice Girl and an abuse survivor, you no longer have to paste on a fake smile to hide your pain and confusion. You no longer have to deny your own needs and opinions to earn the love and approval of others. You don't ever have to again accept physical abuse, manipulation, sexual or financial exploitation, or keep unwanted secrets because you have no other choice. You have survived, you are now safe, and, as Paul mentioned earlier, you can begin to do the soul work necessary to heal from your wounds.

There are many fundamental truths that you'll learn during this soul work, beginning with: The abuse wasn't about you—it was about your abuser. Your abuser is the one with the problem, not you. When this distinction, this truth, takes root in your heart and grows, you will stop taking ownership of what happened. It wasn't your fault. As Shakespeare put it, some people are more sinned against than sinner. Let the sinner, not you, own the sin.

If you are still in an abusive relationship, please read chapter 7 on marriage and the appendix on abuse.

Another essential truth about what happened to you: Most acts of abuse are accompanied by a lie about you, others, and God, that sounds something like, "You aren't important, no one really likes or wants you, and God doesn't love or care about you either." These statements are false—they aren't true because they are lies—and all lies must be exposed and confronted. For most abuse survivors, talking with a trained counselor is instrumental in confronting those lies and healing from the emotional and spiritual wounds inflicted by abuse.*

Moving Forward

Whew, if that chapter hit close to home, it may have been tough to read. It's never easy to think about the trauma that has painfully sifted you or someone else. But you courageously made it to this point, and look at all you have learned. You now know that difficult life experiences, like lacking encouraging words and role models, having anxious parents, and experiencing abuse, can shape girls into adult Christian Nice Girls. You also learned earlier how an incomplete picture of Jesus, as well as the "sugar and spice" pressures from the Nice Girl Culture, can influence you to act more like a Nice Girl than a gracious, firm woman of faith.

Speaking of gracious firmness, are you ready to meet some role model women who embody those qualities? Don't grab your purse and car keys just yet—you aren't going to meet them at Starbucks—you are going to read the next chapter and meet God's Good Women on the pages of his Word.

CNG Nicole

Walking into her parents' house, Nicole sees her father working on his taxes.

"Hey, Dad, are you paying off the national debt?"

Looking up and smiling at the unexpected visit, Nicole's father replies, "I wish. It's good to see you. What brings you by?"

Sliding into a nearby chair, Nicole says, "I came by to pick up something Mom asked me to return to a store near my work."

"Thanks for doing that for her. You know how driving downtown makes your mom nervous. Listen, take a look at these numbers for me. I'm not sure I'm figuring them correctly."

Nicole quickly scans her father's calculations. "Everything looks fine to me, Dad."

"Good. I sure am glad you decided to major in accounting. It's worked out really well for you."

Nicole feels a familiar frustration rising in her, thinking, *I never felt like I had a choice.* "Dad, accounting hasn't worked out so great for me."

Shocked, Nicole's father shakes his head. "How can you say that?! Did you do something wrong at work? Did you get fired?"

"No, no. My job is fine. I meant that sometimes I wonder what it would be like if I had majored in music. You know, my teacher said I could have gotten a scholarship for playing the saxophone."

"Nicole, I never did trust that music teacher. She was always putting big ideas in your head. Besides, that was a long time ago. Why are you bringing this up? It wasn't a good idea then or now. I hope you aren't planning to do something foolish like quit your job and join some band playing in a smoky bar. What would people think?"

Nicole sighs. *Why does he always jump to conclusions? And who are these people that we're always supposed to be worried about pleasing?* "No, Dad. I'm not running off and joining a band. I'm trying to tell you that being an accountant wasn't *my* dream. It's what *you* wanted for me."

"Is it wrong to want what's best for your daughter? There are always jobs for accountants. It's a safe bet. You can't say that for playing the saxophone."

"I know music is not the safest choice, but Dad, don't you ever get tired of always going with the safest, most sensible, most boring choice?" Nicole asks, her voice rising.

"Nicole! What has gotten into you?!" asks her father, aghast at her outburst.

Sighing again, Nicole slumps back in her chair. "I don't know, Dad. I guess I'm just regretting always taking the easy and safe way out. And to be totally frank, I regret that I allowed you and Mom to talk me out of majoring in music. I know you love me and were trying to protect me, but all these years later, I still wonder what could have been. My music was really important to me, and I . . . just gave up. I put that dream on a dusty shelf somewhere."

Patting her hand, Nicole's father stands up. "Honey, some dreams just aren't meant to come true. I'm going to go get your mom to sign these tax forms."

As she watches him leave, Nicole ponders her father's words. *But what if you're wrong, Dad? What if music is what God had planned for me all along, and I missed out because I was afraid to take a chance? The next time God brings an exciting opportunity my way, I'm jumping in with both feet, no matter what the neighbors think!*

Study Questions

1. What purposes do you see behind the painful siftings that God allows in people's lives?

2. Do you think God created you as more of a "coconut" or a "peach" when it comes to how you react to stressful, emotional situations?

3. Who were your female role models when you were a child and teen? What did you learn, positive or negative, from watching them?

4. When you were growing up, did you hear primarily encouraging or discouraging words from adults? How did those words make you feel? What words would have made a positive difference in your life if you had heard them?

5. Review the list of overprotective parenting behaviors that transmit fear to children. Did your parents display any of these? If yes, how did this type of parenting affect you? If you are a parent and display any of these overprotective behaviors now, which one would be the easiest to change in your life?

6. What do you think is the difference between displaying cowardice and having a gentle spirit?

7. Think of some people you know personally who are courageous. What fears are they facing?

8. Where in your life do you need more courage? What are some small steps you could take to face this fear and begin to grow your courage?

9. Do you need to develop/deepen relationships with role model women in your life? What are some initial steps you could take to make that happen?

10. When you are afraid, do you tend to overreact, underreact, or respond appropriately?

11. (This question is private. You will not be asked to share your answers with your group.) Have you experienced verbal, emotional, spiritual, physical, or sexual abuse? What, if any, lies have you believed as a result of the abuse? Do you need to seek help from a ministry leader or therapist?

Bonus Bible Study Question: Read Job 23:10; Psalm 119:67; Jonah 2:2; Zechariah 13:9; Romans 8:28; 2 Corinthians 1:3–7; 4:17; and 1 Peter 1:6–7. Based on these verses, what is the good or the purpose that God can bring out of human suffering?

CHAPTER FOUR

Nice vs. Good: How Does God Prefer His Women?

Pssst . . . come here. . . . Scoot over on the church pew so we can lean in close and whisper a personal question in your ear: "Are you ever-so-slightly tired of hearing Sunday school lessons and sermons lauding the gentle spirit of Mary of Bethany as she sat at Jesus' feet? Yes, she's a wonderful example of making Jesus top priority, but all these lessons and sermons and books on her . . . do they ever make you feel like God must surely prefer women who passively sit, nice and quiet, throughout their lives?"

Good news, girlfriend! God loves a spirited woman who does more than sit with her hands folded as the world crumbles. Mary of Bethany is one of many biblical female role models who pleased God with assertive and courageous actions.* This chapter is full of biblical and modern-day female role models and their gutsy actions. Unlike Christian Nice Girls,

*For the record, Mary of Bethany's refusal to get up and help her sister, Martha, was courageous. If Mary had been a people-pleasing Christian Nice Girl, she would have jumped up the first time Martha shot her a dirty look for sitting.

these are God's Good Women who chose to be good instead of just nice, and subsequently brought God glory and advanced his kingdom. Immortalized forever in God's Word, they prove that God prefers his women to do more than passively sit on their hands while evil triumphs. Many of them were trailblazers who chose risky paths for women.

Deborah: Speaker of Hard Truths

Let's start in the Old Testament with Deborah, a working woman who spoke hard words of truth as she led Israel. You can read her exciting story in Judges 4–5. Deborah's story takes place back before Israel had a king, when the country was led by judges / prophets who functioned much like a governor does today. The Canaanites had cruelly oppressed Israel for years, leaving the Israelites discouraged and despondent, but repentant for their worship of false gods. God responded to their cries for help by giving them Deborah as judge and prophetess. Her name means "honeybee," but she wasn't all sweetness and light. Judges 4:4 identifies Deborah in Hebrew as an *eshet lappidot*, usually translated "wife of Lappidoth." However, some commentators have noted that since there is no biblical record of a man named Lappidoth, and *lappidot* means "torch," that *eshet lappidot* may be better translated as "Deborah, a spirited woman."[1] Don't you love that? She wasn't a Nice Girl, she was a spirited woman—and God loves a firecracker!

Do you work outside the home? So did Deborah—literally. She held court outside under a palm tree a few miles from Jerusalem, judging disputes and speaking for God. She was a pioneer, and no doubt, some people in this patriarchal society were offended that God raised up a woman to lead Israel; however, Deborah was concerned with pleasing God, not making everyone like her. She didn't want to offend God by rejecting his call on her life, so instead she risked offending her fellow citizens. She was true to who God created her to be, and ultimately, the people loved her for it. If you decide to become one of God's Good Women, you will offend someone, guaranteed. But if you stick with it and are faithful to God's call on your life, you will find, like Deborah did, that more people will love you for your authentic self than would ever have loved the people-pleasing you.

Getting back to the story, in response to the Canaanite oppression, Deborah sent for an Israelite military leader, Barak, and said to him, "The Lord, the God of Israel, commands you; 'Go, take with you ten thousand men . . . to Mount Tabor. I will lure Sisera [the enemy commander] . . . with his chariots and his troops to the Kishon River and give him into your hands' " (Judges 4:6–7).

Barak agreed to the task, but only if Deborah would go with him. She agreed to go, but added, "Because of the way you are going about this, the honor will not be yours, for the Lord will hand Sisera over to a woman" (Judges 4:9). Sounds like Deborah is going to get the honors, doesn't it? Wrong—God has another woman in mind, but let's not get ahead of the story. Please note that Deborah just spoke a hard truth to Barak, and she (gasp!) hurt his feelings—actually, she probably devastated Barak because, to a soldier, there was no greater honor than to capture the enemy leader. If Deborah had been a CNG, she would have kept this fact to herself so that Barak wouldn't get mad or offended.

Jael: A Stand-Up Woman

Let's finish up this exciting story. God gives Israel victory in the battle, and the enemy commander, Sisera, runs for his life, right into the tent of Jael, another one of God's Good Women. Are you a home-maker? So was Jael. Judges 5:24 describes her as "most blessed of tent-dwelling women." When Sisera ran to her tent and told her to hide him, she was anything but nice. She invited him in, but while he slept Jael picked up a hammer and drove a tent stake through his head into the ground. She knew that she and her family would be in danger if the Israelites found her harboring the enemy, so she killed him. Now, that's a woman who will stand up for herself and others! A CNG would have allowed Sisera to bully her into lying for him and endangering her family. Doubtless, Jael's heart pounded with fear as she crept toward the sleeping enemy, but that didn't stop her from pounding that tent stake and killing evil dead when it entered her home. God's Good Women are perceptive and proactive like Jael. They aren't passive, which means they don't ignore danger or wait around for things to fall apart before they finally react.

Ruth: Perfumed Risk-Taker

Like courageous Jael, Ruth was a risk-taker who faced fear to save both her and her mother-in-law's life. Ruth's story, found in Ruth 1–4, begins with the deaths of her husband, father-in-law, and brother-in-law in Moab. Ruth was from Moab, but she refused to let her Israelite mother-in-law, Naomi, return to Judah without her, uttering those famous words, "Where you go I will go, and where you stay I will stay. Your people will be my people and your God my God" (Ruth 1:16). Leaving her childhood home, family, and idolatrous faith was risky, but as one of God's Good Women, Ruth didn't shrink back from a challenge. Instead of playing it safe and letting her past dictate her future like Christian Nice Girls do, Ruth boldly put her whole future in God's hands by making a complete break with her past.

The two women settled in Judah with no income and no marriage prospects because Naomi was past childbearing age and Ruth was an outsider. They could have given up and starved to death, but Ruth took the initiative to glean leftover barley in the fields. And as God would have it, she ended up in Boaz's fields. He was a distant relative of Naomi, and after he noticed Ruth's industrious work and noble character, he made sure that she was protected from unwanted male attention and that his workers left plenty of grain for her to harvest.

Now the story gets particularly intriguing. Naomi, playing matchmaker, tells Ruth, "[Boaz is] a kinsman of ours. . . . Tonight he will be winnowing barley on the threshing floor. Wash and perfume yourself, and put on your best clothes. Then go down to the threshing floor. . . . Note the place where he is lying. Then go and uncover his feet and lie down. He will tell you what to do" (Ruth 3:2–4).

A Christian Nice Girl would have refused Naomi's request. Put on perfume and slip around in the dark uncovering men's feet—oh my, what would people say if they found out? And what if Boaz gets the wrong idea and starts playing footsie? A CNG would have stayed home, prim and proper, offered an earnest prayer alone, and hoped that Boaz would magically figure out that this young woman was interested in marriage to a much older man.

Ruth didn't stay home that night; instead, she followed Naomi's instructions completely. When Boaz woke up in the dark, startled to find a woman lying at his feet, he asked, "Who are you?" Don't you imagine Ruth's heart was about to jump out of her chest as she laid it all on the line and replied, "I am your servant Ruth. . . . Spread the corner of your garment over me, since you are a kinsman-redeemer" (Ruth 3:9). The penniless foreigner Ruth was asking wealthy landowner Boaz to marry her. He could have rejected and publicly humiliated Ruth for her boldness, but she didn't let her fear or her past stop her from taking steps to change her current situation. That's what God's Good Women do. They push past their fears and assertively go after what God has for them—sometimes breaking with tradition and convention.

Boaz agreed to marry Ruth, and they later had a son named

Obed, who had a son named Jesse, who had a son named David. Yes, that David—the shepherd boy who became king of Israel. And it all started when one of God's Good Women bravely said good-bye to her past, showed initiative, took risks when God gave her opportunities, and . . . dabbed a little perfume behind each ear.

Abigail: Beauty and the Beast

Sometimes God's Good Women can end up married to fools. That's what happened to beautiful and intelligent Abigail in First Samuel 25. She was married to a wealthy, surly rancher named Nabal, whose name means "fool." Abigail's nail-biter story occurs when David and his men, hiding from King Saul, are camped near Nabal's ranch in Maon. At sheepshearing time, David sent a delegation of his men to ask politely for some food because they had previously protected Nabal's sheep and herdsmen. Nabal, confirming the aptness of his name, ridiculed David and sent his men away empty-handed. When David's men reported what had happened, David was furious, rounded up his men, and set off to kill Nabal and his workers.

A servant told Abigail what Nabal had done and warned her of the impending danger from David. The situation was perilous and frustrating—first, her husband had done something foolish, and now David was planning to do something even more foolish in return. A Christian Nice Girl might have wrung her hands in fear or wasted time complaining about her husband's bonehead actions. A CNG might have done nothing more than "pray really hard about the situation," which, to be painfully frank, is sometimes a way of avoiding making the bold decisions people already know they need to make. A truly confused CNG might even have mistakenly thought that she needed to support her husband's dangerous choices in the name of being a "biblically submissive wife." (We'll talk more about what biblical submission is and is not in chapter 7.)

Instead, Abigail immediately packed up bushels of food and wine, sent her servants ahead with the provisions, and got on her trusty donkey. When Abigail intercepted David, she defused his murderous rage like a seasoned diplomat. She apologized for her husband's churlish behavior and repeatedly called David "my lord" to make up for Nabal's insults. She brought abundant provisions to correct the injustice and ingratitude David had experienced. Then Abigail bravely dared to give David a new perspective on the situation. She reminded him that revenge would be unwise, because as Israel's king one day, he wouldn't want needless bloodshed on his hands. She also urged him to leave vengeance in God's hands.

Abigail was shrewd in dealing with David—just as Jesus commands believers to be in Matthew 10:16—meaning she showed keen awareness, sound judgment, intelligence, resourcefulness, and an intuitive grasp of practical matters. She carefully chose the truths she spoke to David. Unlike CNGs, who equate shrewdness with sin and naïveté with godliness, God's Good Women are savvy. They quickly discern how to best handle a situation to take care of themselves and those under their care.

David listened to Abigail and recognized that God had sent her to keep him from committing murder. When God's Good Women act wisely, God ultimately gets the glory. Abigail saved her family with her bold words and actions, but she also saved David and his men from sin.

When she returned home, she found Nabal partying and too drunk to listen, so she sensibly waited until morning to tell him what had happened. He was so shocked that he had a stroke and died ten days later. There's no record of anyone being particularly saddened by his demise. David, who obviously knew one of God's Good Women when he saw her, later married Abigail.

Lydia: Persuasive Purple Power

Let's move from Old Testament to New Testament women, and start with Lydia in Acts 16:11–15. Her name suggests that she was a former slave, but rather than let her past hold her captive, Lydia worked hard and became a successful merchant of luxurious purple-dyed cloth in a male-dominated business world. She was a non-Jewish truth seeker who was already worshiping God when she first heard the apostle Paul preaching about Jesus. God opened her heart to the Truth, and she became the first Christian convert in Europe.

Grateful to those who taught her about Jesus, wealthy Lydia invited Paul and his three companions to stay at her home in Philippi. Scripture records that Lydia had to urge the men repeatedly until they finally agreed to her invitation, probably because Paul didn't want to be seen as freeloading off new converts, plus there were "strong taboos against Jews accepting hospitality from Gentiles."[2] If Lydia had been a CNG, she would have stopped asking after their first "no thank you" hurt her feelings. A CNG would have taken their rejection personally instead of discerning that this was a time to insist, not shrink back. Sometimes God's Good Women have to be forcefully persuasive, just as Jesus was, despite cultural pressures to be quiet and timid.

Also, note that Lydia's "good work" of offering hospitality was not motivated by fear. Many CNGs believe that God always needs appeasement, so they sacrifice and "serve" him, not out of love, but out of fear of his disapproval or rejection. Good works motivated by love produce joy, freedom, and mutual benefit, and they come with no strings attached; good works motivated by fear sometimes produce resentment and often come weighed down with strings of expectation. Neither the producer nor the recipient of fear-prompted good works receive the best God has for them.

Lydia was also shrewdly thinking ahead by offering hospitality to these missionaries—she and her household would have additional time with them to receive more teaching and truth. Can't you see her gathering everyone around the breakfast table, salting the scrambled eggs while peppering Paul with theological questions? Lydia was willing to forcefully persuade these Jewish men to go against "the rules" and accept her Gentile hospitality so that she and her household could have the pleasure and benefit of learned teachers under their roof. In contrast, CNGs are over-focused on following "the rules" and needlessly give up pleasures in order to earn God's love. They fear that if they step outside their culture's rules, God will drop them like last season's hot fashion trend—if they aren't perfect, God won't want them.

Lydia knew, as God's Good Women know, that this is no way to live. Eventually this treadmill spirituality will wear you—and those around you—out. God doesn't expect perfection—he wants good women who are motivated by deep love for him and who aren't afraid to make a few mistakes along the way. It takes a while to become one of God's Good Women, and in the process you learn that you can't avoid every mistake or please everyone. There simply isn't time to be that uptight and rigid. God designed limits to your time, treasure, and talents so you wouldn't squander your life away. Recognizing your limited time here on earth can motivate you to say, "Good-bye, perfectionism, I don't have time for you!"

Priscilla: Hanging With the Boys

A few chapters over from Lydia, you can find Priscilla in Acts 18. She and her husband, Aquila, met the apostle Paul in Corinth after being forced to move when Claudius Caesar decreed that all Jews had to leave Rome. As one of God's Good Women, Priscilla refused to wallow in misery over her forced deportation, and instead got busy making tents (and converts) with her husband and Paul.

Priscilla was a gutsy woman. She hosted a church in her home, and was open to adventure, traveling with her husband and Paul, and even risking her life for Paul at one point (Romans 16:3–5).

In her day, the Jewish religious leaders did not consider women worthy of teaching.[3] As a trailblazer, Priscilla not only soaked up as much teaching as she could from Paul, but also taught what she learned to a man. If she had been a CNG, she would have allowed her culture to keep her totally quiet. Once, while in Ephesus, Priscilla and Aquila heard an eloquent, enthusiastic preacher named Apollos boldly teaching in the synagogue to repent because Jesus, the Messiah, would appear soon. His fervent message was not inaccurate or insincere—it was just incomplete because "he knew only the baptism of John" (Acts 18:25).

Priscilla and Aquila didn't correct him publicly, which would have embarrassed Apollos and confused the listening Jewish audience. Instead, they met with him privately and, with gracious firmness, affirmed where Apollos was correct, and then taught him the rest of the story (Acts 18:24–26). God's Good Women speak the truth, but they know how to correct errors without losing the person in the process. Rather than despising or criticizing people for what they don't know yet, God's Good Women share the truth they know, and then leave the results up to God. Women like Priscilla understand that they are responsible for speaking the truth in love, not for making people accept the truth. CNGs often don't speak the truth because they are afraid that other people will reject or criticize them. That's an excuse, not a valid reason for remaining silent.

Fortunately, Apollos did accept the truth Priscilla and Aquila taught him, and doing so enabled him to have a powerful ministry in Corinth (1 Corinthians 3:6; 16:12). Priscilla helped both Apollos and Paul become even more effective in their ministries. Paul commended her and Aquila as "fellow workers in Christ Jesus" and added that "all the churches of the Gentiles are grateful to them"

(Romans 16:3–4). On this particular thank-you list, Paul even listed Priscilla's name before her husband's—an unusual occurrence in Bible times—which may indicate that Paul considered her the more prominent Christian worker.[4] Priscilla's decision to teach Apollos was revolutionary two thousand years ago, and in some churches today, still controversial and displeasing to believers who focus exclusively on 1 Corinthians 14:33–35 and 1 Timothy 2:11–15. Whether you agree or disagree that women should teach the Bible to men, please know that like Jesus, God's Good Women follow *him* rather than the rules.

Other Tough and Tender Women of Faith

You may be aware of the praise given to the late Mother Teresa, winner of the Nobel Peace Prize. But did you know that she was dogged throughout her life by criticism? It's hard to believe that anyone would dare to criticize her, but criticism follows almost everyone who decides to be good instead of merely nice. Christopher Hitchens, rogue journalist, cynic, and harsh critic of faith in general, has called Mother Teresa the "ghoul of Calcutta," and her Missionaries of Charity a "cult of death and suffering," in his documentary *Hell's Angel*. Yet she rose above her critics because she understood that Christianity is not a religion comprised of only sweet and gentle virtues. She wrote, "I have found the paradox, that if you love until it hurts, there can be no more hurt, only more love." Mother Teresa, as one of God's Good Women, understood that showing Christ's love to the world comes with hurt, but she also knew that by persevering, believers can turn their hurt into even more love.

To the slaves she helped rescue, Harriet Tubman, former slave, abolitionist, humanitarian, Union spy during the Civil War, and women's suffrage advocate, was a near mythological figure with exceptional strength, courage, and ingenuity. She was beaten and whipped as a little girl. Early in her life, she suffered a traumatic head wound when she was hit by a heavy metal weight thrown by an irate overseer. The injury caused disabling seizures and powerful visions. A devout Christian, she ascribed her visions to God.

She believed that her difficult life experiences, along with her mother's Bible stories, were put in her life to help others gain their freedom. But in order to do so, she would have to discard sentimental spirituality and fight like God's Good Women do. On the verge of being sold into slavery once again, she decided to run away. "There was one of two things I had a right to, liberty or death; if I could not have one, I would have the other. For no man should take me alive. I should fight for my liberty as long as my strength lasted, and when the time came for me to go, the Lord would let them take me."[5] Tubman would later help hundreds obtain their own freedom from slavery.

Sojourner Truth was the self-given name of Isabella Baumfree, who was also an African-American abolitionist. She was born into slavery and sold around the age of nine for a hundred dollars to a man who beat and raped her. Late in 1826, Truth escaped to freedom. She later became a devout Christian and traveled and preached against slavery and capital punishment and advocated for women's rights and prison reform. She was met with fierce opposition. During her speeches, people booed, interrupted, and tried to belittle her with the contemptuous accusation that she wasn't even a woman. The spirited, near six-foot-tall woman proved her accusers wrong by opening her blouse and revealing her breasts!

She worked to improve the conditions of African-Americans and met with President Lincoln. Critics and enemies mounted, but like all people who stop being nice and start being good, she gained supporters and influential friends, including William Lloyd Garrison and Susan B. Anthony.

Several days before Truth died, a reporter interviewed her as she lay "weakened by pain and suffering." Her last words to her interviewer were, "Be a follower of Jesus."[6] Teresa, Tubman, and Truth followed the real Jesus of the Bible, the 360-degree Savior who did more than bring us salvation. He also brought protection, rescue, and a real-world example of what love is, how we should really live, and what is worth living and dying for. Like their Savior, these women were gracious and firm, sweet and salty, and at times blessedly inappropriate. (We don't recommend opening your blouse to prove your gender. Best to keep them guessing.) And like Jesus—like all of God's Good Women—they changed the world around them.

God's Good Women inspire young and old, male and female. I (Paul) received great insight and motivation from their lives as I founded The Protectors, an organization that provides both faith-based and value-based solutions to adolescent bullying. The Protectors rescues children from the injustice and cruelty of bullying by providing courage training; however, The Protectors would never have been born if I had failed to see the crucial difference between just being nice and being good. If I had stuck with Krispy Kreme Christianity, I would be offering bullied children only a shoulder to cry on. While that is helpful, it's not enough. They also need heroic people of faith—like Deborah, Abigail, Mother Teresa, Harriet Tubman, and yes, you, if you choose to become one of God's Good Women—to defend human dignity. Peace, for the oppressed and broken, is not created through warm and fuzzy thoughts, but through the active, bold pursuit of justice.

This chapter's title asked a question: "How does God prefer his women?" The answer rings out in his Word and throughout history: God likes his women with a firm will that aligns with his will. Strong, courageous women who get in line with the will of God are destined to change their corner of the world.

93

CNG Nicole

Trapped in a boring committee meeting at church, Nicole surreptitiously checks her watch under the table and thinks, *I can't believe we have been debating napkin colors for fifteen minutes!*

"The mother-daughter tea is always in the spring, so women will be expecting pastel-colored napkins!" says the women's ministry coordinator.

Another committee member sighs. "But we always do pastel colors! Let's try something new and bold, like teal and brown."

Elizabeth, a recent addition to the committee, speaks up. "If we want to do something truly new and bold, how about we change more than the napkin colors? Have you noticed that the neighborhood around our church is becoming more multicultural while our congregation is not? We have an international mission field at our doorstep. This year, why don't we do something different? We could have mother-daughter teams visit neighboring homes and invite them to a fun outdoor event."

Nicole is intrigued. *What a great idea! Elizabeth is such a trailblazer.*

The coordinator frowns. "But we always do a mother-daughter tea, Elizabeth. It's a tradition."

"I'm not suggesting we throw out the whole idea. Let's just tweak it and use it as a way to get mothers and daughters involved in ministry to our surrounding neighborhood. Our purpose stays the same, but we go about accomplishing it in a different way."

Another member pipes in. "That might be dangerous. The neighborhood has gone downhill."

Nodding her agreement, the coordinator says, "Yes, we wouldn't want to put our women in any kind of danger."

The neighborhood is not downtown Beirut! I need to say something, but it might make the other women uncomfortable. Despite her heart pounding,

Nicole interjects, "It's not like there are drive-by shootings every day. The neighborhood is safe, but even if it wasn't, is that a reason for us to ignore it? Maybe we need to shake things up and take some more risks if we are going to be a truly Christ-centered ministry to women."

Eight heads swivel to stare at Nicole.

Elizabeth speaks first. "Nicole, I am tickled to hear you say that. We do need to take more risks."

Ann, the oldest committee member, adds, "It seems like we do the same thing year after year. Not that those things are bad, mind you, but it's good to do something fresh. Keeps the mind sharp and the spirit dependent on God. I like this idea."

The coordinator, looking puzzled, says, "Well, I guess we could consider changing things up. Elizabeth, Nicole, and Ann: Do you three want to discuss this possible event and report back at the next meeting?"

The three women exchange smiles and nod yes.

"Fine, then let's move on to our next agenda item. . . ."

Nicole settles back in her chair, heart still thumping, but pleased with her show of courage and spirit. *Wow, I said something! And now I get to work with Elizabeth and Ann. They seem like really great women— godly and gutsy. Who knows? Maybe we'll get to be good friends. My life will be richer with more friends like them.*

Study Questions

1. Like Deborah, have you been true to who God has called you to be? Has this offended other people?

2. Like Deborah, do you obey when God tells you to speak a hard truth to someone? What can hold women back from speaking the truth?

3. Jael killed evil dead when it entered her home. In what ways could evil enter your home (e.g., magazines, words, people, etc.)? How could you be more proactive in confronting evil in your home?

4. Ruth didn't let her fear, her past, or tradition stop her from taking bold steps to change her current situation. Are you allowing something from your past to dictate your future? Are you shrinking back from a challenge? How could you boldly put your whole future in God's hands?

5. Ruth showed godly initiative in a risky situation. Where do you need to take more risks when God gives you opportunities?

6. Abigail was shrewd and quickly discerned how to best handle a dangerous situation that threatened her and her family. What steps do you need to take to become more savvy and resourceful like her?

7. Like Lydia, are you able to be forcefully persuasive when necessary, or do you tend to shrink back? Where in your current life are you being timid?

8. What do you think motivates your good works: love for God or fear of God's rejection/disapproval? Do you ever feel like you have to be perfect or God will drop you?

9. Priscilla was able to correct someone else's errors without losing the other person in the process. When have you experienced similar success? Share with your group any tips you have for speaking the truth while simultaneously maintaining a good relationship.

10. When do you think it is okay for Christian women to "break the rules" as Mother Teresa, Harriet Tubman, and Sojourner Truth did?

Bonus Bible Study Question: Read 2 Kings 22:11–23:3. What actions and attitudes did Huldah display that proved she was one of God's Good Women?

CHAPTER FIVE

Friendships and Family: How Nice Wrecks Your Relationships

Puzzled, unhappy, and tired, Christian Nice Girls sit across from me (Jennifer) on my counseling office couch every week with the same basic question: "What am I doing wrong?" They try really hard with their friends and family but usually end up feeling drained and angry instead of fulfilled. It doesn't make sense, does it? These women are clearly sowing physical and emotional energy in their relationships, so it seems like they should be reaping meaningful, satisfying interactions left and right. After all, the Bible says in Galatians 6 that people will reap what they sow. And yet one after one, CNGs say the same thing:

"I feel like my friends/family take advantage of me. As a Christian, am I supposed to turn the other cheek and let that happen?"

"My family doesn't appreciate me, and I lose my temper with them way too much. I feel like a terrible Christian when I get so angry."

"Sometimes I just want to run away from everyone."

The Bible isn't wrong—people do reap what they sow—but

sometimes they misunderstand what will grow from what they sow. For example, if you want flowers flourishing in your flower bed, don't plant weeds instead of zinnias, or you are going to be disappointed at what pops up. Likewise, if you don't like what's sprouting up in your relationships, you need to look at what you are sowing with friends and family. You're probably planting weeds and hoping for flowers.

"But wait," you might say, "I'm not sowing weeds with my ungrateful family and friends! I'm as nice and helpful as I can be to them. I practically kill myself doing for them, and you should see how little I get in return." Yes, that's the point. Those nice behaviors, when taken to an extreme and when done out of fear of rejection, conflict, or criticism, *are* weeds in relationships.

Christian Nice Girls don't understand this fact. They sow false niceness in their relationships, hoping that this will produce intimacy and connection. But false niceness can never and will never produce an authentic, deeply meaningful relationship, just like weeds won't magically produce zinnias.

Planting Weeds

Let's examine Christian Nice Girls' relationships and discover when they plant the undesirable weed of false niceness. Upon meeting a new person, CNGs are usually pleasant. So far, so good. Then, at some point, the other person does or says something that they don't appreciate or shouldn't agree to, and instead of speaking the truth with love and grace, CNGs act nice. Why? Because acting nice feels natural—so natural that it's hard to detect its hidden, selfish payoff: It allows women to avoid uncomfortable but necessary conflict, and it permits them to chicken out of doing the challenging work of establishing healthy boundaries with gracious firmness.

Here are some real-world examples of planting false niceness:

Joe: "Could you lend me three hundred dollars? My car is going to be repossessed unless I come up with some money. I'll pay you back next month."

CNG: *(thinking) I'd have to get a cash advance on my credit card to lend him money, and I've heard he often has money problems.* "I'm not sure I can swing that this month. Three hundred dollars is a lot of money."

Joe: "I could probably scrape together half of it if you could come up with $150. Can you at least swing that amount?"

CNG: *Well, maybe I could get a $150 cash advance. I don't want to seem tight-fisted and unchristian. Plus, he'll be so disappointed with me if I refuse.* "I guess I could come up with $150. But I really need you to pay me back."

Joe: "Don't worry, I'm good for it."

And guess who is still waiting to get her money back because CNGs can be alarmingly naïve about the real motives of abusive people? This CNG planted the weed of false niceness and reaped financial hardship. She also harvested feelings of self-recrimination and even shame because, deep down, she suspects that she allowed someone to steal from her, and stealing is a sin. Oh, and she has a bumper crop of resentful, angry feelings over being used. But because she's a CNG, she's likely to deny all these negative feelings because good Christian women don't get angry, right?

Here's an example for all the Christian Nice Daughters out there:

Mom: "I just got off the phone with your aunt. She said that you are planning a vacation to Hilton Head next summer. When were you going to tell me this?"

CNG: *I'm not five years old! I don't have to report my every move to my mother!* "Oh, I guess I forgot to mention it."

Mom: "Well, it's humiliating when other people have to inform me—your mother—about what is going on in my own daughter's life. I had to pretend like I knew all about your vacation plans. How do you think that made me feel?"

CNG: *This is crazy! I am not to blame because Mom chose to lie, but she wouldn't talk to me for days if I said that.* "I'm really sorry. Next time I'll let you know earlier."

Mom: "I hope you will. You put me in a very awkward position."

CNG: *How does everything always end up being my fault?* "I'm sorry that happened to you. I'll keep you better informed in the future."

Then the bewildered Christian Nice Daughter stews over this confrontation for the next week, replaying it in her mind and thinking of all the zingers she could have thrown in Mom's face—followed by feeling guilty for wanting to zing some zingers at Mom. She sowed false niceness with Mom and reaped false guilt and unrealistic expectations.

Now a final example:

CNG: "Do you think I should audition for the choir? Most people that I've asked tell me I should give it a try."

Friend Debbie: "You aren't thinking you're going to get any solos, are you? You don't exactly have a solo-quality voice."

CNG: *What a mean thing to say! I never said I was a great singer.* "I know I'm not that good of a singer. I just thought it might be fun to sing in a choir."

Friend Debbie: "Are you sure the choir director accepts members like you—you know, people who don't know anything about music and are looking to just have fun? I bet he gets irritated with people like that who waste his time goofing off during choir practice."

CNG: *I do too know something about music. She's making me feel like an idiot! But she might get offended if I say that.* "I'm not sure what the director is looking for."

Friend Debbie: "Well, maybe you should find out before you audition for the choir, Miss Beyonce."

You can probably guess who never joined the choir and who never gave her sharp-tongued friend needed feedback so Debbie could overcome her mean-girl ways and become more like Christ. This CNG planted false niceness and reaped a harvest of demeaning insinuations and sarcasm.

A Tale of Two Paths

Looking back over these examples, can you detect the dangerous pattern in a CNG's interactions with friends and family? She doesn't speak the truth, even when she thinks it! She chooses to ignore the long-term harmful consequences of smothering the truth and instead focuses on the short-term comfort of false niceness. Everyone faces a similar fork in the road in relationships: Do you choose the "act nice" route, or do you choose the path of truth and to be real and risk rejection instead?

The "fake nice" road looks deceptively smooth at first and oh, so Christian. CNGs choose this way, just going along to get along, aiming to keep everyone happy in a misguided attempt to follow Christ (whose sandals never took one step on this particular path). Travelers on this misleading trail try to stay safe and warm by knitting themselves a comfy pullover of seemingly convenient half-truths. Okay, lies. But like a wool sweater worn on a sweltering August hike, these lies eventually make you itch and sweat emotionally, particularly when the "fake nice" path inevitably gets rockier as resentment and dissatisfying, even dangerous, relationships pile up.

In contrast, the road of authenticity and truth looks intimidating at first. It can seem like a steep climb to risk disappointing other people or making them mad by being honest and firm—but this straightforward route gets easier over time and leads to self-respect, righteousness, and true intimacy.

It's a fact: Conflict is the price you pay for intimacy. Read that sentence again, and let it sink in. If you want to connect genuinely with other people, you have to risk conflict by being frank and firm

NO MORE CHRISTIAN NICE GIRL

in addition to gracious and loving. It's that salty and sweet combination again. And though not a popular message, risking conflict by speaking the truth in love is part of following Christ. This is what the real Jesus modeled for us. He didn't avoid necessary conflicts if those interactions could possibly lead to a more authentic, intimate relationship, and he always spoke the truth in love.

Speaking the Truth With Love and Grace

If you are looking for modern-day examples of what it means and doesn't mean to speak the truth in love and grace, look no further than the hit show *American Idol*. The show began with three judges who, probably not coincidentally, represented three basic personality types. Paula Abdul represented the more passive personality. Her comments toward amateur singers were cordial, but not always truthful. Her uncertain voice and fidgety body language revealed how uncomfortable Paula was with providing honest, constructive criticism. Fortunately, she progressed and found the courage to be more truthful, even when doing so earned her an occasional boo from the audience.

Aggressive Simon Cowell is truthful, but oh my, his cutting, callous comments make us wonder if *American Idol* provides crisis counseling to the many contestants whose young souls are assaulted by him. Simon demonstrates how being truthful without love is like performing surgery without anesthesia: It gets the job done but causes unnecessary pain and suffering. Simon speaks the truth aggressively, without love or graciousness. But like Paula, he's changed through the years and has learned to soften some of his harsh comments in order for them to be more helpful.

Then there's the "Big Dawg," Randy Jackson. He's the assertive personality type that is good at being truthful and loving at the same time. His graciousness prepares his listeners' ears to hear what he has to say so they can improve their performance. Assertiveness puts other people at ease with grace, love, and care. Interestingly, Randy hasn't changed much through the years. He's basically the same person, and that's a good thing.

Randy also doesn't permit the potential boos of the audience to deter him from speaking the truth and disagreeing with the crowd. At times, being assertive does involve disagreeing with others; however, that disagreement can be done in a way that is not *needlessly* confrontational and painful.

Planting Truth

To illustrate this type of assertiveness, let's replay some of the uncomfortable situations provided earlier in this chapter, and put you, the reader, in the driver's seat. But this time, unlike the CNG, imagine you risk some conflict by speaking the truth in love and grace while retaining your dignity and integrity. As an added bonus, you're going to give others important feedback they need for their own personal growth.

You: "I've been considering auditioning for the choir."

Friend Debbie: "You aren't thinking you're going to get any solos, are you? You don't exactly have a solo-quality voice."

You: *That was kind of rude, but maybe she's just having a bad day. I'll give her the benefit of the doubt.* "I didn't say I was looking for a solo. I enjoy music and think it would be fun to sing in a choir."

Friend Debbie: "Are you sure the choir director accepts members like you—you know, people who enjoy music but don't know anything about it and are looking to just have fun? I bet he gets irritated with people like that who waste his time goofing off during choir practice."

You: *Forget the benefit of the doubt. She puts me down almost every time we are together. It's time to say something.* "Debbie, you may be unaware of this, but it's hurtful and discouraging when you make comments that suggest I don't know much about music or that I would goof off during practice."

Friend Debbie: "Oh. Well . . . I didn't mean to hurt your feelings. I just didn't want you to be disappointed if the choir audition didn't work out. I guess I said it the wrong way."

You: "Thanks for acknowledging that, and for your concern for me."

And Debbie wanders off, slightly miffed at what just happened but also wondering if she needs to rein in her tongue in the future. She might even make the previously unseen connection between her cutting comments and her shrinking number of friends. Overall, she responded fairly well to the truth assertively spoken in love. The next example demonstrates a worst-case scenario.

Joe: "Could you lend me three hundred dollars? My car is going to be repossessed unless I come up with some money. I'll pay you back next month."

You: *I'd have to get a cash advance on my credit card to lend him money, and I've heard he often has money problems.* "It's hard to tell a friend no, but I don't have the money to lend, and I also generally don't lend people money."

Joe: "But I am really in a bind! I will lose my job if I can't drive. I could probably scrape together half the money if you could come up with $150. Can you at least swing that amount?"

You: *He's really pushing me hard to lend him money. He's going to get mad when I stick to my guns.* "Joe, I know you are in a bind and that you really need your car. But I can't lend you any money."

Joe: "I thought you were my friend! I would help you out if you were desperate."

You: *I hate situations like this, but I'm going to be firm.* "We are friends, but I don't appreciate it when you pressure me to do something that isn't a good choice for me. Please stop asking me to lend you money."

Joe: "Fine! I guess I'll just walk ten miles to work every day. Some kind of Christian you are!"

And Joe stomps away, angry and disappointed.

And yes, when a worst-case scenario happens, you may feel kind of yucky afterward—a mixture of guilt, anger, and sadness—but if you dig a little deeper, you will uncover some good feelings sprouting up too, such as relief, self-respect, and integrity—and they will blossom and grow, especially when you get your credit card statement. Those positive feelings are only found when you take a risk and choose the path of truth.

Keep digging deeper and you'll discover that what you thought was guilt isn't guilt at all—it's *false guilt* masquerading as the real thing. You feel real guilt when you do something that is actually wrong. But it's not wrong to refuse to lend money you either don't have or don't think is appropriate to lend. It's actually wise. However, when you are first learning to say no with conviction, you may feel uneasy and nervous as you practice using your firm no, similar to how you might feel practicing your beginner's Spanish on a trip to Mexico. Knowing about this troubled feeling in advance will help you not to mislabel your "beginner's nerves" as justified feelings of guilt. Thankfully, every time you speak the truth in love, you will feel stronger and grow increasingly comfortable with your new way of communicating.

People Teach You Who They Are

After you speak the truth in love to people, pay close attention to their response because they are teaching you who they are and what you can expect from them in the future. Overall, people tend to fall into one of three response categories: spiritually mature, "getting there," and immature. Spiritually mature people will receive loving truth well and even thank you for your courage and caring. They are Proverbs 27:6 people: "Faithful are the wounds of a friend, but deceitful are the kisses of an enemy" (NASB). Spiritually mature people appreciate that loving truth can sting at times, and they prefer it over fake flattery, which doesn't help anyone grow. If you cultivate relationships with them, you are sure to reap bushels of blessings, such as an equitable give-and-take, accountability, and genuine concern for your well-being. You'll grow stronger and feel more peaceful and comfortable in your own skin.

"Getting there" people will receive loving truth in a mixed fashion. They might be displeased or disappointed initially, but after some time, they respect what you said and don't make you pay a lengthy emotional price for your honesty. It takes them a while to get there (hence their name), but over time, they show themselves to be people who are attempting to value truth and respect boundaries. They are Ecclesiastes 7:25 people: "So I turned my mind to understand, to investigate and to search out wisdom in the scheme of things and to understand the stupidity of wickedness and the madness of folly." "Getting there" people are trying to learn; they are imperfect but teachable. If you cultivate relationships with them, you will reap mostly blessings with an occasional pesky weed.

Immature people will not receive loving truth, no matter how gently you offer it. You can agonize over what to say, endlessly rehearse your future conversation, and then deliver your pearls of wisdom in a tone more tender than Florence Nightingale—and in the end, it won't help. The immature want what they want, when they want it, and how they want it, even if having what they want damages you. They act like demanding, careless two-year-olds (hence their name) and are Jeremiah 9:5 people. "Friend deceives friend, and no one speaks the truth. They have taught their tongues to lie; they weary themselves with sinning." Spiritually immature people wear themselves (and their friends) out with their foolish choices and words. If you cultivate close relationships with them, you will harvest truckloads of trouble, such as repeatedly being lied to, taken advantage of, and disrespected.

You Teach People How to Treat You

When you accept delivery on truckloads of disrespectful treatment, you are teaching immature people that they can continue to misuse you. When you allow the immature to dictate the terms of relationships, you are giving them the green light to exploit, neglect, or abuse you. Isn't it sad how women can see this happening in other people's relationships but can be so blind to being misused in their own relationships?

Or perhaps they recognize the exploitation but mistakenly defend doormat behavior by quoting Jesus when he taught: "You have heard that it was said, 'Eye for eye, and tooth for tooth.' But I tell you, Do not resist an evil person. If someone strikes you on the right cheek, turn to him the other also" (Matthew 5:38–39). Be careful how you interpret this passage because Jesus is teaching here that people shouldn't retaliate with harmful words or actions of their own when they are harmed by others. Simply put, don't seek revenge, but do seek to create healthy boundaries with other people. Self-defense of your body, emotions, and possessions—and the defense of others—is not the same thing as seeking revenge. God's Good Women have the freedom to protect what is valuable while also having the responsibility to steer clear of the sin of revenge. Jesus did not seek revenge, and he had excellent boundaries. He did not preach or daily live a doormat gospel. He protected what was valuable and didn't allow himself to be disrespected and abused until doing so had a divine purpose at his crucifixion.

Prior to his garden of Gethsemane surrender, Jesus never let the spiritually immature control or misuse him. Early in his ministry, the hometown crowd, angered by his speaking, took Jesus "to the brow of the hill . . . in order to throw him down the cliff." Jesus did not accept their physical abuse; instead, "he walked right through the crowd and went on his way" (Luke 4:29–30). In Luke 13, when a synagogue ruler indignantly protested that Jesus should have waited until the Sabbath was over to miraculously heal a crippled woman, Jesus didn't accept this ridiculous rebuke and ask, "Please may I have another?" Instead, he answered, "You hypocrites! Doesn't each of you on the Sabbath untie his ox or donkey from the stall and lead it out to give it water? Then should not this woman . . . be set free on the Sabbath day from what bound her?" (vv. 15–16).

This is just one of many instances where Jesus taught the religious leaders that they couldn't treat him disrespectfully and expect him to take it lying down. This partly explains why the religious leaders decided to arrest Jesus under the cover of night and bring along a detachment of soldiers. Past experience with Jesus had taught them that he wasn't afraid of necessary conflict. They knew he was no doormat.

Avoid the Fool's Game of Changing the Immature

What are people learning from their relationship experiences with you? Firmly speaking the truth in love and maintaining healthy boundaries in relationships will teach most people to treat you respectfully. However, not everyone is teachable, and ultimately, you aren't responsible for how people accept your truth spoken with love and grace. Your responsibility is to simply put it out there for consumption, much like parents putting vegetables on the dinner table. Parents are responsible for offering healthy foods, but ultimately children decide whether they will swallow what's good for them. Spiritually mature and "getting there" people will consume what's good for them in relationships, even if it doesn't taste good going down, but the immature will not.

If someone is not teachable, you will completely waste your time and energy if you try to teach them what they aren't interested in learning or changing. They aren't in a relationship with you to grow and develop; instead, they believe they can use you to meet their own needs regardless of whether you are harmed in the process. They have soul work to do, such as developing empathy, humility, and other virtues that are best taught by God. In other words, pray for them, get out of the way, and let God get to them. He will orchestrate life lessons that will teach them what they need to know.

Hang On to Your Hat

Before the chapter ends, here's one last question for you: Does it seem like your crop of friends contains almost no spiritually mature people, only a handful of "getting there" people, and bushels of immature people? If your relationships consist primarily of spiritually immature people who are treating you poorly, either you teach middleschoolers or (brace yourself) you are not as spiritually mature as you think you are. Yes, that's right: If you find yourself constantly surrounded by spiritually and emotionally immature friends, then you probably fall in that category yourself.

Ouch—but true. People tend to be attracted to people who are similar to them. When nines on the spiritual maturity scale are looking for intimate friendships, they aren't drawn to threes. Nines often have threes in their circle of acquaintances and offer love and guidance to them, but rarely are they sister-close. If you want to cultivate deep friendships with mature Christians, you have to start by becoming more spiritually mature yourself. It's like playing tennis. A really good player will occasionally play with a beginner, but in order for the experienced player to be challenged and to improve, she is required to play most frequently with people who are at or above her skill level. If you don't like who you are hanging out with, then it's time to step up your own game instead of complaining about the quality of player who will agree to play with you. If you will consistently speak the truth in love and display gracious firmness, you will grow in maturity and find that you are attracting a healthy crop of spiritually mature friends.*

This chapter has focused on how to cultivate your relationships with friends and family. Are you ready to get even more personal? No, it's not time yet for the sex chapter. First you've got to find Mr. Right and get married, so turn the page and learn how false niceness can make dating a disaster.

*Thank you for accepting that final criticism.

CNG Nicole

Driving to the mall to meet her mother, Nicole mentally reviews what she's learned about speaking the truth in love in relationships. *I've never acknowledged it fully, but I have lied to people because it seemed easier. I even thought my lies were making me a better Christian—how mixed up is that?! I've got to stop planting weeds in my relationships.* Flashing blue lights and sirens interrupt her thoughts as she drives up on an accident scene. A police officer directs her to detour off the main road. Nicole concentrates as the detour twists and curves, taking her away from the mall. Finally, she arrives and notices her frowning mother seated on a bench at the mall's entrance. Nicole is barely within earshot when her mom starts in with "I've been waiting for twenty minutes! Where have you been?" Resentment stirs inside Nicole as she remembers the many times her mother has kept her waiting, but she politely replies, "I'm sorry you had to wait. There was an accident, and the police rerouted traffic to a confusing detour."

Sighing heavily, her mother says, "You could have called me. I wasn't sure whether you were going to show up."

Before Nicole can utter the false assurances that spring immediately to mind, the truth gives her a mental two-by-four wallop: *She's packing my bags for a guilt trip, but I didn't do anything wrong. I'm at that fork in the road, and I am so tired of choosing the fake nice path.*

Taking a deep breath to steady her nerves, Nicole replies, "It would have been unsafe for me to call while driving. I'm here now, so let's enjoy our time together."

Her mother, momentarily caught off guard by Nicole's matter-of-fact reply, quickly recovers and declares, "I don't know that I can have a good time now! You've sent my blood pressure through the roof by making me worry about what had happened to you."

Nicole mentally reminds herself not to get hooked into making false apologies and assurances she can't keep, and despite the flutters in her stomach, states, "I understand that you were worried and upset, but sometimes things like this happen. I'm hungry for lunch. If you want to join me, we can head down to the food court."

Her mother, puzzled by Nicole's calm responses, tries one more time. "I hope I can eat. My stomach is in knots."

She can either choose to be immature and go home huffy, or she can get over it and go shopping with me, Nicole realizes. *I'm moving on.*

"Mom, did you hear a Starbucks opened in the food court?"

And to Nicole's surprise, her mother replies, "I did. Everywhere you look there are changes in the mall."

I don't believe it! She gave up on the guilt trip! Maybe she's in the "getting there" category of people. This gracious firmness stuff really works!

"Yes, the mall is changing a lot." Nicole pauses, and smiling inwardly, silently adds, *So am I, Mom—so am I.*

Study Questions

1. What types of weeds have you seen Christian women plant in relationships in the name of being nice? Are you planting false

niceness weeds in any relationships in your life? What were you hoping would grow and what is sprouting up instead?

2. What do you think are the hidden, selfish payoffs for false niceness in relationships?

3. What do you think happens to women's hearts when they repeatedly sow false niceness in relationships?

4. Why do Christian women sometimes choose the fake nice path over the path of authenticity and truth?

5. What do you think are the costs and the benefits of choosing the path of truth and authenticity in relationships?

6. Why do you think some women can see exploitation and abuse when it occurs in other people's relationships, but may be blind to being misused in their own relationships?

7. Prior to reading this book, what was your understanding of Jesus' teaching to "turn the other cheek" in relationships? How does your understanding compare with the actual behavior Jesus displayed in his relationships?

8. Have you tried to teach someone who is not teachable? Share with your group any lessons you learned.

9. Why do you think it is particularly hard for Christian women to accept that some people, at certain points in life, choose not to be teachable?

10. How could you "step up your game" and become more spiritually mature and attract healthier friends?

Bonus Bible Study Question: Read Psalm 53:1; Proverbs 10:18; 14:9; 15:5; 18:6; 20:3; 26:11; Jeremiah 4:22; and Acts 28:27. According to these Scriptures, what characteristics and behaviors are typical of the spiritually immature? What word does the Bible use frequently to describe someone with these characteristics?

CHAPTER SIX

Dating: How Nice Attracts Mr. Wrong

Have you met Mr. Wrong? He can look deceptively similar to Mr. Right, but behind his smile lurk trouble and heartache. When Christian Nice Girls are single and dating, their people-pleasing tendencies can attract Mr. Wrong like sugar attracts flies. You'll learn in this chapter how to swat him away when he comes buzzing around, as well as dating tips that will help you find Mr. Right.

Attracting Mr. Wrong

Doesn't it seem like Christian Nice Girls would attract Mr. Right? After all, CNGs are mannerly, appear ever so gentle and compliant, and smile until it hurts. Surely those qualities would attract a decent guy. Some CNGs do end up with Mr. Right—glory hallelujah!—but often, that's not what happens. Like the smell of blood for a shark, a CNG's passivity and inability to say no are powerfully attractive to Mr. Wrong. He's a "user." He may not be using illegal substances, but he definitely uses women to meet his own needs—for self-importance, money, sex, reputation, power, etc. And like a shark, he doesn't care who gets hurt when it's feeding time. He knows, from years of experience, that CNGs are easy prey who won't fight back, stand up for themselves, or maintain healthy boundaries.

Some married women are haunted by the ghost of Mr. Wrong. Whether they dated him once or for years, being used by Mr. Wrong can leave women devastated and vulnerable to further misuse. Even if you end up marrying Mr. Right, the harmful effects of previously dating a user can negatively impact your marriage.

Red Flags

All that is scary, isn't it? Rest easy; there are red flags that you can look for to help you identify Mr. Wrong before he sinks his teeth into you. Let's start with your first interactions with a potential dating partner, whether that's at work, in a social setting, at church, or on a blind date. Does he display any of these red flag behaviors?

- He talks quite a bit more than he listens, or he puts no effort into the conversation and expects others to do all the talking.
- His favorite topic is himself. He rarely asks about you.
- When the conversation shifts away from his life, he quickly brings it back to himself.
- He is often the hero of his own stories.
- He makes frequent critical comments about others or jokes at their expense.
- He laughs at, belittles, or ignores your opinions, ideas, or activities.
- He is flamboyant, loud, and boisterous in inappropriate settings.
- When his mistakes are brought to his attention, he gets angry or shuts down, even if the correction is done appropriately.

- When good things happen to other people, he seems to resent it or tries to "one up" them.
- He exaggerates his accomplishments and fudges the truth if doing so will benefit him.
- He flirts or acts seductively with many women.
- He frequently "checks out" women's body parts or makes lewd jokes.
- He spends his money to impress others.
- He regularly ignores laws and regulations, even if doing so inconveniences or endangers other people.
- He gets offended easily.
- He gets angry quickly and without much provocation.
- Once he gets in a bad mood, he stays there, sulking and pouting.
- He dismisses other women's assertions that he is bad news, a player, or a jerk.

The above behaviors are a shark fin sticking out of the ocean. They indicate danger—get away from this guy, even if his physical appearance is as unthreatening as Mr. Rogers, because Mr. Wrong comes in all shapes and sizes. He can be short or tall, well-educated or a high school dropout, a city slicker or a farm boy, and yes, he can be a Bible-toting, Scripture-quoting churchgoer. Mr. Wrong can even be in the ministry.

Regardless of their outward appearance, Mr. Wrongs share the uncanny ability to manipulate Christian Nice Girls. These men know that some women won't push back, are easily led, and will gradually come to accept their selfishness, immaturity, and, in far too many relationships, verbal or physical abuse.

Some Christian Nice Girls naïvely assume that sensitive men are safe, but Mr. Wrong can use his sensitivity to help him be even more manipulative—so don't immediately entrust yourself to a guy just because he cries at sad movies. Some CNGs rule out masculine men because they think that manly strength isn't Christlike. Be careful with this mistake as well. Jesus worked with his hands as a carpenter. He spent a lot of time outside and on fishing boats. Jesus was plenty masculine.

Remember: People teach you who they are, so stand back and observe a guy over time, without trying to change him. Dating is the time when you are supposed to examine men and discover both their strengths and weaknesses, so don't feel guilty or judgmental when you begin to recognize his problem areas. That's how dating is designed to work.

Read over the red flag list again, but this time, imagine that it was someone else's boyfriend who was displaying those behaviors. Wouldn't you think he was a jerk? Often, Christian Nice Girls can identify Mr. Wrong when he's attached to another woman, but they have difficulty identifying users that swim into their own dating pool. This is partly due to the cultural pressure women experience to be nice, accommodating, and never angry in their own personal relationships. The Nice Girl Culture trains them to ignore the subtle (and obvious) cues they pick up that this is Mr. Wrong.

If You See Red, Then Run

As you learned in chapter 2, God gave women brains that can quickly read danger signals. Christian Nice Girls tend to ignore those "something's not right here" signals they get from their intuitive brains because they mistakenly believe that those signals are being judgmental or are somehow unchristian. Ironically, because Jesus commands Christians in Matthew 10:16 to be "as shrewd as snakes and as innocent as doves," CNGs are actually being unchristian when they ignore the red flags and intuitive signals that could lead them to wisely discern that a Mr. Wrong has just surfaced.

Christian Nice Girls also forget that they can and should leave dating situations that are quickly becoming volatile. And the media—a huge part of the Nice Girl Culture—doesn't help them date more wisely. Movies and television repeatedly portray female characters remaining in foolish, dangerous situations and trying to reason with men rather than getting out of Dodge and to safety. Don't follow the typical movie heroine's example—if you sense danger in a dating situation, get out. Don't worry about appearing rude or hurting anyone's feelings. Just get out of there.

If you are frustrated that you're consistently attracted to Mr. Wrong, take a look at your childhood. As discussed in chapter 3, being raised by people who were emotionally distant or abusive can leave you vulnerable to relationship problems later. Sometimes women unconsciously choose Mr. Wrong because being misused is all they know. These women don't enjoy being taken advantage of, but being misused is familiar at least—a known quantity. Sadly, being attracted to Mr. Wrong often results when a woman feels defective at her core: If she believes that she is unworthy and unlovable, then she won't expect men to treat her with dignity and respect, and she will accept poor treatment as her due.

If any of this is ringing your bell, please make an appointment with a trustworthy counselor or minister. Just make sure that you see someone who respects women, highly values human dignity, and shows mercy and grace while also taking a firm stance on sin. If this counselor or minister shames you for wanting to be treated with dignity and respect, wave good-bye and find a more mature Christian to talk to. You deserve to believe, deep down in your bones, that you are a treasured daughter of the King. And once you believe that, you're more likely to be attracted to a prince than to Mr. Wrong.

It's a Date—Not a Requirement

If Mr. Wrong asks you out, don't be a Nice Girl and say yes to avoid hurting his feelings or making him angry. If you don't want to go out with a guy, even a genuinely good guy, don't lie to him. It's lying to pretend an attraction that you don't feel. Speak the truth in love. Say something like, "Thank you, but I'm not interested in dating you." You don't need to try and let him down easy by adding in the dreaded phrase, "Let's just be friends." If he's a good guy, you'll be friends anyway. If he's Mr. Wrong, he may misinterpret that phrase as "Keep pursuing me and eventually you can wear me down." Also, don't tell a man, "I like you, but it's not God's will for us to date / God doesn't want me to date you," to avoid taking personal responsibility for your own choices. It's cowardly to make God the bad guy, plus your pious excuses could mess with his faith.

Tips for Dating Mr. Right

Let's move on to talking about dating Mr. Right. So, you've been watching this guy for a while, no red flags have immediately jumped out, and you decide to try dating him. Don't relax just yet. Here are a few tips to keep in mind:

Tip #1: Date for potential friendship. If something more develops, that's great; if not, oh well, you were looking for friends anyway. When I (Paul) was in college, this was one of the best pieces of advice that I ever received. When you start a new dating experience with friendship in mind instead of courtship, it takes the pressure off and makes your date much more fun.

You can also be more natural, more authentically "you." When dating for potential friendship, you won't feel like you have to be perfect and polished. You can let men know who you really are while also not divulging too much private information. And friendship is the best foundation for a romantic relationship, if one should develop.

The "date for potential friendship" approach doesn't guarantee you pain-free, mistake-proof dating, but it's far better than approaching every first date as the beginning of an unending chain of events that leads to "You may now kiss the bride." In short: Stop being deadly serious about dating (which isn't attractive anyway), and start having fun meeting new friends.

Tip #2: You don't owe your date complete candor and access to your life. Yes, it's crucial to speak the truth in love, but that doesn't mean that you spill your guts, particularly on the first few dates. Retain some sense of mystery about yourself. Christian Nice Girls, in an effort to be well-liked and compliant, are prone to volunteer too much private information and to answer private questions they shouldn't. If your date asks you a private question that you don't want to answer, then politely decline to answer. You can say, "I'm not comfortable answering that question right now" or, "I like to get to know people better before I share private information like that."

Tip #3: Ask and answer meaningful questions that are personal, but not private. You want to get to know him better, and you also need to note if he shows an interest in you by asking similar questions in return. Examples of personal questions include:

- "What makes you happy/sad/angry?"
- "What do you like to do for fun?"
- "What's your family like? What's your relationship with them like?"
- "What's your dream job?"
- "What are your short-term and long-term goals?"
- "What is your relationship with God like?"
- "What makes you feel the closest to God?"
- "When have you felt the closest to God?"

Private questions need to be asked before you agree to marry someone, but not on the first few dates. Examples of questions that are both personal *and* private include:

- "How much money do you make?"
- "Has anyone ever cheated on you?"
- "Have you had sex before marriage? If so, why?"
- "What is your biggest regret in life?"
- "Who made you feel the best and worst about yourself as a child?"

Tip #4: At an appropriate time, tease your date about something he would find funny. This shows that you have a sense of humor and are not completely beholden to his approval.

Tip #5: Be careful not to go overboard with God talk. Remember that you aren't going on a date to learn more about God—you are there to learn more about the other person so you can decide if you want another date. Also, some Christian Nice Girls use theological discussions as a way of avoiding personal (not private) discussions, which ultimately is a way of avoiding intimacy.

Tip #6: If you disagree with something your date says or does, disagree agreeably. For example, "I see that issue differently. I think . . ." is preferable to lying ("I completely agree") or becoming belligerent ("How could you see it that way? That doesn't make any sense.") Remember: Conflict is the price you pay for intimacy. Conflict can be intimacy in disguise, so instead of running from disagreements, learn to approach them like Jesus did. When Christian Nice Girls learn to fight like a Christian, with both love and firmness, their relationships deepen and expand. And if your conflicts with a particular dating partner don't lead to greater intimacy and instead repeatedly rip at the relationship (and your self-esteem), you two are likely incompatible. You tried dating this person, and now it's time to move on.

Tip #7: In advance, decide on your boundaries for physical intimacy and then hold the line. Christian Nice Girls' people-pleasing tendencies can lead them to compromise their own limits. For example, a typical CNG may decide, "Kissing is fine, hugging is fine, but no petting over or under clothes." And then, there he is. Cute, funny, sweet, and . . . turned on. His hand begins the initial descent into the "No Go" zone and what does the CNG do? She begins the mental gymnastics: *Did he mean to put his hand there? Does he realize what he's doing? Should I say something? What if I'm wrong and I end up embarrassing him? I won't say anything. Well, no, that was no accident—he definitely put his hand there. I'll just kind of knock his hand away casually, and he'll get the idea to back off. There. That should let him know to back off.... I can't believe it. He thought I meant to put his hand someplace else even more alarming! This is moving way too fast for me, but I can't say anything now, or he'll think I'm a big tease. Plus I really like this guy. And all this touching does feel kind of good. But I know I'm going to regret this later. Oh man, now he's really turned on. It's too late to stop things. He'd be so angry if I put the brakes on now. I don't want to deal with that conflict. I'll just keep going. I can't believe I'm doing this.*

This doesn't happen only to teenagers. A Christian Nice Girl at any age can find herself in a similar situation. Speak the truth up front about your physical boundaries. Yes, it feels awkward to discuss such private matters, but if you don't, then you may be really angry at and disappointed with yourself the next morning. And if your date won't respect your limits and keeps pushing for more physical intimacies, then he's a Mr. Wrong who slipped in under the radar. Show him the door.

Tip #8: If a man asks for another date but you aren't sure whether you want another one, say, "I will get back to you on that." Then be true to your word, and get back to him after you decide. Remember that dating or courtship is designed to provide you with many exits, many opportunities to say, "This isn't working for me." Christian Nice Girls often stay in unsatisfying or unhealthy dating relationships because they don't take advantage of the following built-in courtship exits:

- The first date: These are designed to help you decide if you would like a second date, but there is no requirement to have another date. Exit at will.

- Multiple dates: These are designed to help you decide if you want to date this man exclusively, but there is no requirement to agree to an exclusive relationship. Exit at will.

- Exclusive relationships: These are designed to help you develop a closer relationship and determine if you could have a future together. But there is no requirement that you remain in the relationship, even if you have been dating for years or if he wants to continue dating you. Exit at will.

- Engagements: These are designed to help you prepare for marriage, but there is no requirement that you must marry your fiancé. Exiting is more challenging now, but it's still an option.

All of these exits are built into the system to give you the chance to say no. Why? Because marriage is one of the biggest decisions of your life, and you want to be married to the right kind of person. These exits give you the freedom to say at any point in a dating relationship, "Thanks, I'm flattered, really, but no thanks. I wish you well in the future." If a man you're dating doesn't want to understand or accept this, then he must have skipped Dating 101—and it's not your job to teach it to him.

So now you know how to spot a shark-finned Mr. Wrong and how to successfully navigate the dating waters. Wait a minute . . . are those wedding bells ringing in the distance? Another Christian Nice

Girl just got hitched. Turn the page, and you'll discover how false niceness can turn a blushing bride into a Desperate Nice Wife.

CNG Nicole

Entering the women's bathroom at work, Nicole notices that Lauren, a younger employee, quickly turns away, but not before Nicole sees her tearstained face and red nose.

"Lauren, are you okay? What's wrong?"

Reluctantly turning back around, Lauren says, "It's so stupid! It's not even worth talking about."

"Well, I respect your privacy, but I'm also willing to listen if you want to talk."

Lauren sighs. "It's not that I don't want to talk about it. It's just that I feel so dumb about what happened."

Nicole thinks, *Here's where I would normally blurt out false reassurances to try to make Lauren feel better. This time I'm going to be different.* Nicole smiles, and silently waits for Lauren to make her choice.

Lauren blows her nose. "Maybe it would help to get someone else's opinion. Here's the deal: I met this guy named Derek in our singles group at church. He seemed like a nice guy, but after a few dates, things started to change. Last night he was checking out other women in the restaurant and making comments about their bodies. It made me really uncomfortable, but when I told Derek that, he got all mad and would hardly speak to me the rest of the evening. I feel bad that I made him mad, but I also feel like I didn't do anything wrong. I'm so confused."

Nicole listens, thinking to herself, *I spy a shark fin circling around.*

"Lauren, a man who respects you—and women in general— wouldn't make lewd comments in front of you. Or pout all night because you called him on it."

Sniffing, Lauren says, "Yeah, I know. I just really like him. He was so nice on our first and second dates."

"Perhaps he was trying to impress you at first, but by the third date, he probably thought you were hooked enough that he could show you his dark side and you wouldn't object."

Peering into the mirror to fix her runny mascara, Lauren adds, "I know he was kind of a jerk last night. But do you think that's who he truly is? I mean, maybe he was just in a bad mood or stressed out."

"Even if he was stressed out, do you want to date someone who treats you that poorly every time he has a bad day?"

Lauren shakes her head. "No way. I dated a guy like that before, and it was a roller coaster. One week he was sweet to me, and then the next week it was like he was mad at me. I never could figure out what I had done wrong."

"You probably didn't do anything wrong. He just needed someone to blame so he wouldn't have to fix whatever the real problem was. He was Mr. Wrong instead of Mr. Right."

Sighing, Lauren asks, "Why do I always seem to end up with Mr. Wrong? Maybe I should just move to a deserted island."

Laughing gently, Nicole puts her arm around Lauren. "I wouldn't pack my bags just yet. Come on, let's eat lunch together and talk some more about finding Mr. Right."

Study Questions

1. Review the Mr. Wrong red flags. Why do you think some Christian women ignore these warning signs? Do you think women ever ignore these signs intentionally?

2. Have you ever been on a date with someone who displayed red flags? How did you respond?

3. If you have dated a Mr. Wrong, how did that dating relationship affect you at the time? Does it affect you now? Share with your group any lessons you learned.

4. What kind of dating scenarios are (or were) hardest for you to exit from?

5. Do you have a history of dating Mr. Wrongs? What do you think contributes to this issue? What steps could you take toward developing more discernment and choosing more wisely?

6. Review the Tips for Dating Mr. Right. Share any successes you may have had with them so others in your group can learn from your victories, past or present.

7. If you are currently dating Mr. Wrong, take some time to pray about this relationship, individually and with your group. Do you need to talk to a mentor, ministry leader, or counselor about this relationship?

Bonus Bible Study Question: Read 2 Samuel 13:1–20. Based on this passage, what red flag attitudes and actions do you recognize in Amnon? How could this tragic but true story help you as you date?

CHAPTER SEVEN

Marriage:
How Nice Messes Up Matrimony

So you've found your Mr. Right. You have our best wishes and this warning: False niceness can mess up a marriage. But before we show you the mess and how to clean it up, it's time for another quiz! It's written for wives, but you could apply current or past dating relationships to the questions as well.

Are You a Desperate Nice Wife?

True	False	My husband tells me that I do too much for other people.
True	False	I almost never spend any money on myself.
True	False	I rarely feel better after my husband and I try to talk things out.
True	False	If my husband does something that bothers me, it's just easier not to mention it.

True	False	I suspect my husband doesn't respect me very much.
True	False	I put a lot of energy into figuring out how to fix my husband.
True	False	I'm so busy taking care of everyone else that there's never any time for me.
True	False	If I'm irritated with my husband, I let him know by sighing loudly, withdrawing, giving him the silent treatment, or making snippy comments.
True	False	I'm putting off going to see a medical or mental health professional about a personal concern.
True	False	I get frustrated when my husband doesn't pick up on my subtle cues that indicate how I am feeling or what I want him to do for me.
True	False	I think my husband is selfish for taking some time to go work out, engage in a hobby, etc.
True	False	It really bugs me when I do something nice for my husband, and then he doesn't do what I want him to do in return.
True	False	We argue frequently over petty stuff.
True	False	Sometimes I wonder if my husband thinks I'm boring.
True	False	Even though I didn't like doing it, I've looked at porn with my husband to make him happy.

If you marked true to five or more questions, you've let dangerous behaviors slip into your marriage that will gradually smother the life out of it, much like kudzu does to trees. Drive through parts of the southern U.S., and from a distance the hillsides will look lush and green. Up close, you'll notice that an invasive leafy vine called kudzu has covered every tree, shrub, telephone pole, and hitchhiker for miles. During the Great Depression, the government supported widespread planting of kudzu to prevent soil erosion, not realizing that this nonnative plant would spread like wildfire and block trees from getting sunlight.[1] What the government initially thought would be helpful turned out to be harmful over the long run. The same process happens with the passive, people-pleasing behaviors of Christian Nice Wives. They think denying their own needs, stuffing their anger, and avoiding necessary conflict will help prevent erosion of their marriage, when these behaviors actually prevent marriages from growing and becoming healthier.

Ignoring Your Own Needs

Let's look at the first Christian Nice Wife behavior that may have kudzu-invaded your marriage: ignoring your own valid needs. Often, a CNWife will disregard her own need for help, rest, exercise, fun, etc., because she focuses exclusively on meeting her husband's perceived needs. Her fear of conflict and rejection drives a CNWife to numb herself to her own legitimate needs so that she can overextend herself to do what she thinks will make her husband happy. Her spiritual training conspires against her as well, having subtly told her that having human wants and needs is somehow worldly, selfish, and even unchristian. Sadly, her choices often harm herself and sometimes even backfire and hurt her husband and family.

For example, a wife might refuse to get some exercise or go to a movie with friends because leaving the kids in her husband's or a babysitter's care makes her feel guilty, or because her husband complains about watching the kids for even a couple of hours. Like all humans, she legitimately needs exercise and fun, but she ignores these needs so that she doesn't have to work through her feelings of false guilt or confront her husband about his unreasonable complaints. It just seems easier to stay home. The end result? She neglects her physical and emotional health, she becomes increasingly dour and burned-out, and she stockpiles resentful feelings. Her husband misses out on opportunities to grow as a parent, deepen his relationship with his children, and bless his wife. Both husband and wife lose . . . and she was just trying to be nice.

Outwardly, a Christian Nice Wife's choice to deny her own needs can make her resemble a self-sacrificing, loving wife, but inwardly, what's really going on? Self-sacrificial acts that are motivated by true love always have the other person's best interest at heart (even if those loving acts might cause either person to experience some necessary pain). Self-sacrificial acts that are motivated by fear of conflict/ rejection and desire for approval may look beautiful from a distance, but look closely and you'll see that they are actually kudzu-covered "covert contracts." That's when a wife does something nice for her husband with the unspoken expectation that he will be just as nice in return. And then when he isn't, she gets angry that he didn't jump through her invisible hoop, and punishes him by sulking, making snippy comments, or giving him the cold shoulder. Covert contracts are manipulative, and they confuse and anger spouses. Most important, they are not what Jesus expects from his followers.

Fool's Gold

Christian Nice Wives change the Golden Rule—"Do unto others as you would have done unto you"—into the Pyrite Rule—"Do unto others so that they will do the same unto you." It's a subtle difference that Jesus explains in Luke 6:31–33:

> Do to others as you would have them do to you. If you love those who love you, what credit is that to you? Even "sinners" love people who love them. And if you do good to those who are good to you, what credit is that to you? Even "sinners" do that.

The 360-degree Jesus sets the bar high for believers. Treat other people the way you would like to be treated—with authentic, loving goodness—because that's what pleases God, not because doing so will guarantee niceness from others in return. Jesus doesn't guarantee reciprocated kindness from your husband or anyone else, including children. He also doesn't want you to be a silent, anxious doormat for your husband or children to wipe disrespect and unkindness on. Both husbands and wives sometimes need to make sacrifices for the good of their marriage, but your love for God, not your fear of disappointing or angering your husband, should motivate any acts of self-sacrifice.

It's also important to be clear that God is the one who is prompting your self-sacrifices. If you're ignoring your own basic needs for any other reason, you are eventually going to resent your husband, particularly when he meets his own legitimate needs. Case in point: Both you and your husband need a nap. He chooses to take a nap while you choose to clean the house, a task that could wait. He wakes up an hour later, refreshed and willing to vacuum, but by then you're so mad you could spit. You chose to disregard your own valid need for rest, and now you deeply resent that he chose to meet his need for rest instead of ignoring his own needs like you did.*

*No, we don't have a camera in your house.

Anger and Conflict Issues

Speaking of resentment, let's move on to the other Christian Nice Wife behaviors that can do a kudzu-creep into your marriage: stuffing anger and avoiding necessary conflict. CNWives are uncomfortable with their own anger. From the Nice Girl Culture, and perhaps from their church and their upbringing, they have learned that expressing anger in relationships is a no-no. And yet, they do get angry and want the situations that prompted their anger to be addressed. So what do they do?

Well, many times, a Christian Nice Wife expects her husband

to be a mind reader who can magically figure out what she's angry about without her having to directly explain it. Yes, she may express frustration by slamming the kitchen cabinet doors, but if he asks her, "Honey, what's wrong?" he's likely to hear, "Nothing!" God didn't give men highly intuitive brains—he gave that type of brain to women, so you are asking your husband to do something extremely difficult if you expect him to notice and intuitively figure out what you or anyone else is feeling. For example, have you ever gone to a party and been disturbed by the underlying tension between another married couple? Then, when you get back in the car, you say to your husband, "Whew, things are tense between those two!" And he replies, "What? I didn't notice anything."* He's mystified, and you can't believe he would miss something so obvious.

*No, we don't have a camera in your car either.

That's just how the typical male brain works, which means you will be continually disappointed if you expect your husband to intuitively read your mind so that you don't have to own your own feelings. A Christian Nice Wife often wants to avoid the discomfort of owning up to her anger and her needs and wants. After all, the Nice Girl Culture, outside and inside the church, pressures her to bury her anger and needs so that she will be deemed a perfectly Nice Wife. When assertively expressing your needs or your anger in a constructive manner is equated with being demanding, owning up to those needs or angry feelings can seem too costly; however, that's what God's Good Women do. They take a risk and speak the truth in love about what they want and need and what makes them angry. Then, they listen (to the other person and to God), negotiate, speak some more truth, listen again, and so on.

Taking the initial risk to assertively express themselves is particularly challenging for Christian Nice Wives who come from dysfunctional families or are abuse survivors. These painful experiences train women to believe that no one will meet their needs or respond appropriately to their anger, so why even say anything? Likewise, being married to a foolish or abusive man (like Nabal from chapter 4) can make owning and expressing your emotions feel like wasted effort. If these are your experiences, please go talk to a trusted mentor or counselor who will encourage your efforts to own and express your needs and feelings.

Buried Treasure

Now, don't think that Christian Nice Wives never express angry feelings—because many of them do. The problem is *how* they choose to express their anger: Either they bury valid concerns and get angry over little things instead, or they express their anger in indirect ways. Do you find that you and your husband argue intensely over the most minor things? Whether it's how to load the dishwasher properly or whose mother makes the best mashed potatoes, CNWives will snip and snipe over inconsequential matters in an effort to avoid discussing bigger, riskier issues like trust, power, respect, love, etc. A CNWife might be angry because her husband won't say no to any outside requests for his time, but when he finally gets home, she's more likely to pick a fight about how he trimmed the hedges than to acknowledge her loneliness and feelings of unimportance. That would be too real and too risky for a CNWife who has yet to learn that conflict is the price she must pay for intimacy.

Christian Nice Wives might also bury valid marriage concerns in a misguided attempt to fulfill 1 Peter 3:1–4. They may believe the "gentle and quiet spirit" praised in this passage means that they should muffle their authentic self, as if wives who hide their hearts under a heavy wool blanket please God the most. But the passage actually reads:

Wives, in the same way be submissive to your husbands so

that, if any of them do not believe the word, they may be won over without words by the behavior of their wives, when they see the purity and reverence of your lives. Your beauty should not come from outward adornment, such as braided hair and the wearing of gold jewelry and fine clothes. Instead, it should be that of your inner self, the unfading beauty of a gentle and quiet spirit, which is of great worth in God's sight.

This passage instructs Christian wives on how to handle being married to an unbelieving husband: Don't preach at him repeatedly when he has already heard the gospel and is unresponsive. He's not listening to your spiritual words anymore; instead, be a living example of the gospel for him. An unbelieving husband is much more likely to be won over by your inner transformation into the image of Christ than he is your outer adornments or theological debates. And your inner transformation has to include all 360 degrees of Christ—his sweet, gentle side that knew when to remain silent and his assertive, frank side that knew when to speak up. What does that look like in a marriage? You keep quiet about the hedges (they'll grow back), and you speak the truth in love about how lonely, unimportant, and angry you feel when he puts time with you at the bottom of his priority list.

Wipe Your Feet, Please

Let's move on to the other problematic way that Christian Nice Wives express their anger: indirectly. Do you ever bang pots around and slam cabinet doors when you need help in the kitchen and your husband isn't volunteering? Or make purchases that exceed your family budget and then hide them from your husband?

These are indirect ways of expressing resentment and anger that stem from "doormat syndrome." When women don't assert themselves properly and instead let others walk all over them, they resent it, either consciously or unconsciously, and stockpile unexpressed angry feelings. Those resentful feelings that weren't expressed in the original situation will tumble out and be expressed indirectly in other situations, leading to unpredictable explosions over minor annoyances or to subtle, passive-aggressive expressions of "you're not the boss of me" messages.

No wife wants to identify herself as passive-aggressive, but any woman who believes that Christians should be "sugar and spice and everything nice" 24/7 is going to build up an imposing stockpile of simmering anger. And that festering resentment is rocket fuel for passive-aggressive responses in marriage and other relationships.

If you have difficulty identifying passive-aggressive responses in yourself or others, here's what to look for: Aggressive behavior obviously harms the other person (e.g., yelling, hitting). Passive-aggressive behavior is less obvious but still harms others because necessary or agreed-upon actions aren't performed (that's the passive part) in order to get back at someone (that's the aggressive part). Examples of passive-aggressive behavior in relationships include *repeated* instances of:

- Lateness
- Procrastination
- Forgetfulness
- Sullenness
- Stubbornness
- Refusal to comprehend
- Resistance to suggestions
- Intentional withholding of needed information
- Talking behind someone's back
- Hostile sarcasm*

---

*This list also describes your average fourteen-year-old.

These annoying behaviors allow Christian women to fight against unwanted expectations without paying the price of open conflict. In marriage, these passive-aggressive actions allow a Christian Nice Wife to maintain her outward façade of niceness while also getting back at her husband. Pretty cool trick, huh?

Here are other ways a Christian Nice Wife expresses resentment and anger indirectly:

- Rolling her eyes in contempt or sighing loudly when she doesn't agree with her husband instead of respectfully discussing their differing opinions.

- "Forgetting" or procrastinating on an agreed-upon task her husband wants done instead of risking conflict by openly admitting she doesn't want to do it and then negotiating.

- Complaining to her girlfriends about her husband instead of addressing her concerns directly with him.

- Ignoring the clock and making her husband late for an event that she didn't want to attend instead of directly stating her preferences and discussing the event.

- Refusing to stick with an agreed-upon budget and hiding purchases or extra cash from her husband instead of renegotiating the budget with him.

If you want to break free of doormat syndrome, you need to pinpoint the specific situations where you are avoiding necessary conflict, either in your marriage or other relationships. Wherever you feel the most insecure and fearful is probably where you're being the most passive. Then, practice speaking the truth in love and being appropriately assertive and firm. Here's some language you could use in the above situations:

- "My opinion on this matter is different from yours. We are either going to have to agree to disagree, or schedule some more time to talk and find our common ground."

- "I understand you think it's important for me to accomplish that task, but I have no interest in doing that at this time. Let's brainstorm and see if we can find a solution."
- "I felt angry/hurt/embarrassed/lonely/sad/afraid when you did _____. Let's talk about the situation."
- "I enjoy spending time with you, but I don't want to go to this event because _____. Let's talk about it."
- "Our budget doesn't give me enough money to buy the things I need and occasionally buy something I want. Let's look at the numbers again together."

Being comfortable with asserting yourself is a crucial part of reflecting all 360 degrees of Jesus, because healthy assertiveness and godly submission go hand in hand. You can't have one without the other. Christ displayed both, and he expects the same from his followers.

The Big Question

Sooner or later, almost every Christian wife that I (Jennifer) counsel asks the Big Question: "What do you think it means to be biblically submissive?" These wives have heard the First Peter 3 passage quoted earlier, or the following Scriptures, and want to know what obeying them specifically looks like.

> *Submit to one another out of reverence for Christ. Wives, submit to your husbands as to the Lord. For the husband is the head of the wife as Christ is the head of the church, his body, of which he is the Savior. Now as the church submits to Christ, so also wives should submit to their husbands in everything. Husbands, love your wives, just as Christ loved*

*the church and gave himself up for her to make her holy. . . .
In this same way, husbands ought to love their wives as their
own bodies. He who loves his wife loves himself. . . . Each one
of you also must love his wife as he loves himself, and the wife
must respect her husband.*

Ephesians 5:21–33

*Wives, submit to your husbands, as is fitting in the Lord.
Husbands, love your wives and do not be harsh with them.*

Colossians 3:18–19

You may have heard different interpretations of these passages, ranging from "neither he nor she is the final authority" to "her opinion counts, but he gets the final vote on really big decisions" to "she should keep her opinions quiet and support all of her husband's decisions, whether she likes them or not." Christian Nice Wives are often looking for precise Scripture interpretations because they are afraid of making a mistake and angering God or of not living up to the CNWife expectations their church, husband, extended family, etc., may have for them. CNWives want a guaranteed no-fail Biblically Submissive Wife recipe to follow.

Guess what? We aren't going to give you a step-by-step recipe, for a couple of reasons. First, each marriage has its own "flavor," so a rigid, "no substitutions" recipe wouldn't work for your unique relationship. The Bible provides godly principles that husbands and wives have to apply and work out in their individual marriage based on their personal strengths, weaknesses, background, talents, stage of life, etc. For example, let's say the wife is a stockbroker and the husband has no interest in financial planning. Should he automatically be required to make all the final decisions about where to allocate their 401(k) funds simply because he's the husband? No, that would be an unwanted burden on him and a waste of her God-given abilities.

Second, you won't get a Biblically Submissive Wife recipe because you (and your husband) need to do the challenging spiritual work of figuring out who God wants you to be in your marriage. In order to shape you into the image of Christ, God may want you to either speak up or listen more, take more risks or show more caution, or express your anger more openly (yet without sinning) or keep a tighter rein on your temper. The list could go on and on, just like the transformation process goes on and on for believers. And few things have the tremendous potential for powerful transformations that marriage does. You can fake being Christlike for a few hours at church, but the daily blessings and pressures of living with your spouse will reveal where you are spiritually strong and where you have a lot of spiritual work to do.

Figuring out who God wants you to be in your marriage requires that you submit to God first because he is the highest authority. Christian Nice Wives who believe that pleasing their husband is the same thing as pleasing God make the mistake of making their husband the highest authority. Husbands, like all humans, are capable of making some mighty bad decisions. If you ignore what God, your intelligence, and your intuition are telling you because you think it would please God for you to blindly follow your husband, you are sadly mistaken and headed for disaster.

Twisting Scripture

One final note on biblical submissiveness: After counseling hundreds of Christian wives and husbands, I (Jennifer) have noticed that very few Christian husbands complain about their wives having a submission problem. Many husbands in troubled marriages report that they would like for their wives to be less bossy or controlling, but they rarely label bossiness as a spiritual problem with submission. A wife may, in fact, have a problem with constantly telling her husband what to do, but the average Christian husband doesn't use First Peter 3 and

Ephesians 5 to berate his wife about her controlling behavior (nor should he).

In contrast, I have observed that the minority of Christian husbands who do harp on their wives about their supposed lack of submission are often men who are emotionally, verbally, spiritually, and/or physically abusive. These men pull out Scripture and use it as a whip to humiliate and control their wives. With verbal "sleight of hand," this kind of husband uses God's Word to distract his wife from noticing that the real problem is not her alleged lack of submission—the real problem is his abusive words, attitudes, and actions. To learn more about this subject, please see appendix B.

After applying what you have learned in this chapter about being more honest, assertive, and truly loving inside your marriage, it's time to apply those same lessons inside your bedroom. Get ready, girlfriend—here comes the sex chapter.

CNG Nicole

"Hey, Mom! Look what I got!" Twelve-year-old Tyler runs into Nicole's bedroom, holding a video game. "It's the newest Madden football game!"

"Wow, that's great! Did you buy that with your allowance?"

Tyler shakes his head. "No, Dad bought it for me. I can't wait to show it to Austin!" Tyler dashes out the door, almost colliding with his father.

"Whoa, slow down, champ!" David laughs.

"Sorry, Dad, I gotta go call Austin!"

As Tyler hurries down the hall, David says, "I knew he would love having that video game on the day it was released."

Nicole thinks, *I know David won't like hearing this, but I need to speak up.* "Honey, I know you were excited to buy that for Tyler, but we talked about how important it is for the kids to learn to budget and save their allowance for things they want to have."

David shrugs. "It wasn't that expensive."

"That's not the point. Tyler needs to learn how to handle money. Plus, you bought him a fishing pole last week, and a skateboard two weeks before that."

"Nicole, you don't have to tell me what I bought my son. And you also don't need to tell me how to spend money," David says, frowning.

Nicole feels her stomach clenching as she hears the irritation in her husband's voice. She reminds herself, *Just speak the truth in love.*

"I'm not telling you how to spend money. I'm reminding you of what we already discussed and agreed upon."

Heading for the bedroom door, David shakes his head and mutters, "Fine. I need to mow the lawn."

Later that evening, Nicole sees David sitting on their front porch swing, staring at nothing. *I'm so afraid he's mad at me. Everything in me is saying to apologize, but I know I didn't do anything wrong. And I'm still upset with him for buying Tyler all that stuff. This disagreement isn't me-versus-him anyway—it's about helping our kids learn an important life skill.*

Joining her husband on the porch, Nicole asks, "Want some company?"

"Sure, have a seat." David scoots over, making room for Nicole, and then continues to swing in silence.

I wish he would say something. My stomach is churning. I bet it would help me calm down if I prayed. So . . . Heavenly Father, I need some help right now. Please give me wisdom, courage, and strength. Help me to know when to speak and when to listen. Thank you. Breathing deeply, Nicole looks out at the setting sun and gradually begins to relax as quiet minutes pass.

David, still staring off into the distance, speaks. "You know, when I was a kid, I rarely got anything new. Most of my clothes and toys were handed down from my three older brothers. That didn't bother me much—I never did care about clothes—and my parents were doing their best to keep us all fed and taken care of. Then, for my twelfth birthday, my parents bought me a brand-new bike. It was black with silver trim, twelve speeds. No one had ever ridden it but me. It was the most amazing feeling to have something new. I guess I just want Tyler to experience that same feeling."

Sliding her arm through David's, Nicole says, "I want that for Tyler too. I just also want him to learn how to manage money."

"I know. That's important too."

Nicole and David continue to swing in companionable silence for a few minutes.

David turns to Nicole and smiles ruefully. "The next time Tyler wants something new, I'll point him toward his allowance instead of my wallet."

"You are a great dad, David Chrisman."

As he strokes Nicole's hand, David replies, "Thanks, honey. You're a great mom."

Nicole lays her head on his shoulder, thinking, *How about that? I guess conflict really can be intimacy in disguise.*

Study Questions

1. Review your score on the quiz. Are you a Desperate Nice Wife (or Girlfriend)? Which of the questions on the quiz were thought-provoking for you? Why?

2. When do you tend to ignore your own needs? How do you feel afterward?

3. Think back over the last month and identify any self-sacrifices

(of time, energy, money, etc.) that you made. Who or what was motivating those self-sacrifices?

4. What do you typically do when you get angry at your husband or boyfriend? Does your behavior reflect the 360-degree Jesus?

5. "Conflict is the price you pay for intimacy." If you have risked conflict in your marriage or romantic relationship by assertively speaking the truth in love, and then experienced a resulting deeper intimacy, share your success story with your group so they can learn from your experience.

6. In the past, how have you interpreted First Peter 3:1–4? If you are married, how has your interpretation helped and/or hurt your marriage?

7. When do you tend to express anger indirectly (in a passive-aggressive manner)? What initial steps could you take to begin expressing your anger assertively and appropriately?

8. What do you think it means for a Christian wife to be biblically submissive? Why do you think this topic often stirs up confusion, frustration, and resentment in Christian women?

9. Is there a particular area in your marriage or romantic relationship where you need to speak the truth in love more often?

Bonus Bible Study Question: Read Psalm 103:8–10; Proverbs 29:11; 30:33; Mark 3:4–5; Ephesians 4:26–27, 30–31. According to these verses, does God get angry? Is anger by definition a sin? Can anger become sinful? If yes, how does that happen?

CHAPTER EIGHT

Sex: How Nice Steals Your Spice

Well, here it is—the sex chapter. This chapter was written to be informative but also fun, because God designed married sex to be fun. Christian Nice Girls, unfortunately, rarely experience sex as fun, freeing, and fulfilling. Outside the bedroom, they might be super-organized homeroom mothers or high-level executives, but inside the bedroom, they often turn into little girls—uncomfortable and awkward.

To illustrate, consider how an anxious first-grade girl would act in an uncomfortable situation—let's say her first day at a new school. Reluctant to enter the room, she worries about how she looks, compares herself to the other girls, and decides that they are cuter. She's quiet and doesn't want to be noticed. She waits for someone else to approach her rather than taking the initiative herself. If the teacher asks her about herself, she gives short answers with a tight, tense smile. If she's invited to play a game that she doesn't enjoy, chances are that she will join in anyway, pretending to have a good time just to make everyone happy. Or she might pretend to be sick so that she can avoid the playground altogether.

Now, let's switch to the bedroom. The anxious first-grader is an adult married woman, but when it comes to sex, she's right back in elementary school. She's reluctant to go to bed at the same time as her husband because he might ask her for sex. She worries about her body: Is this too big, too small? She compares herself negatively to airbrushed sixteen-year-old magazine models, and decides that her husband must be disappointed in her body as well. She changes into pajamas in the bathroom so he won't see her naked. She rarely, if ever, approaches him for sex, even if she is in the mood. Sometimes she even talks herself out of feeling in the mood, telling herself, "You're too tired, and sex is too much trouble." She's been known to fake being asleep or having a headache to avoid sex.

If her husband asks her how he could please her more in bed, she laughs nervously and gives a short, vague answer that frustrates and confuses him. While she may enjoy sex occasionally, she has secretly faked feeling pleasure or having an orgasm. She doesn't consider that behavior as lying since it protects her husband from feeling bad about his sexual performance and keeps her from having to work on developing her own sexual response. That's not her biggest secret, though. She won't ever tell anyone that her husband suggested spicing up their sex life by using pornography together—and that she reluctantly agreed despite feeling degraded inside. She just wanted to make him happy, so she passively went along with the flow instead of assertively creating a mutually satisfying sexual relationship. It's first grade all over again, only the stakes are much higher.

God's Plan for Sex

Did any part of that scenario sound familiar to you? That scene plays out in far too many Christian Nice Wife bedrooms, and it always leads to heartache and disappointment. For wives (and husbands) who replay the above scenario month after month, moments of agonizing desperation occur when they silently ask themselves, *Is this it? Is this all there is to sex?*

No, God had so much more in mind when he designed sex. His plan for your marriage includes a rich, mutually satisfying, soul-connecting, mind-blowing sexual union with your husband. How can you know this is true? Just read the Song of Solomon, also known as the Song of Songs. God devoted this entire book of the Bible to celebrating romance and sex. You won't find a book in the Bible dedicated solely to finances or parenting or careers—but there is a book just on physical intimacy. The presence of Song of Songs and its subject matter confirm the high value God places on pleasurable, spirit-connecting, married sex.

And if God thinks something is very important, then so should you.

Easier said than done, huh? Because of physiology and significantly higher levels of testosterone, the typical husband finds it easy to think that sex is very, very, oh so very important. But the typical Christian Nice Wife? Because of her anxieties over her body and sexuality, she finds it much easier to put sex farther down her priority list, perhaps even near the bottom, right after #43: Brush the dog's teeth. This difference is one of the most common complaints that I (Paul) receive during men's conferences, and it leads to untold sexual frustration in many married Christian men.

Join the Club

If you'd like to see sex move up higher on your priority list, try becoming an enthusiastic admirer—better known as a fan—of mind-blowing, spirit-connecting, just-as-God-planned married sex. And if you're going to become a fan, you'll need a fan club to belong to. Let's call it the CWIVES Club. No, that's not a dance club—it's the Christian Wives Initiating, Valuing, and Enjoying Sex Club.

Although the CWIVES Club doesn't have a clubhouse (unless you're counting your bedroom), it does have an official manual: the eight chapters of the Song of Songs. Written as a love poem, Song of Songs is an intimate story of the love between a bridegroom and his bride. They speak to and about one another throughout the book, describing in heartfelt detail their passionate feelings for each other as well as the ups and downs of their relationship. It's an interesting read, so please put down your copy of *No More Christian Nice Girl*, find your Bible, and quickly scan the Song of Songs. We'll wait while you read. Go on—it's a short book, just a few pages.

So . . . what did you think? Can you believe that book is actually in the Bible? It's hot stuff. Tommy Nelson, pastor and author of *The Book of Romance*, says that the Song of Songs is "eight power-packed, very explicit, and highly practical chapters on the topics of love, sex, and intimacy."[1] Now that you've read the manual, you are cordially invited to become a member of the CWIVES Club, but before you join, you need to know about the club's archenemy: the Voice.

Public Enemy Number One

Oh my, the Voice. It chatters incessantly inside the head of every Christian Nice Wife who feels uncomfortable with her sexuality. The Voice criticizes and taunts. The Voice lies:

- "Your breasts/legs/arms/stomach/bottom are too small/big/fat/saggy."
- "You look stupid in that lingerie."
- "You are never going to enjoy sex, so just give up."
- "Sex is dirty, and so are women who enjoy it."
- "Your husband is a pervert for wanting to have sex."

- "You need to shave your legs and wash your hair, so just forget about sex tonight."
- "It's too embarrassing to ask him to do that/touch you like that."
- "Don't make any sounds when you have sex because that's embarrassing."
- "Sex takes too long and it's too messy. It's not worth the trouble of getting undressed."
- "Pretend you're asleep and he'll leave you alone."
- "You're not doing it right. You just aren't any good at sex."
- "Couples your age/your stage don't have sex anymore. It's no big deal."
- "He's getting bored. He's going to find someone else if you don't agree to look at porn with him."

The Voice is not your friend. The Voice is your enemy—a thief who will rob you of pleasure and steal the joy and soulful intimacy of sex.

The Voice is not your husband speaking. I (Paul) address thousands of married men yearly, and most aren't critical of their wife's body or sexual performance—they are just grateful to have sex on a regular basis, and wish their wives understood how sex makes them feel loved and valued.

The Voice is not God speaking. When God speaks about your body and married sex, he sounds like the Song of Songs—celebratory, encouraging, pleased—not critical, condemning, and fearful.

If you are going to enjoy and fully enter into sexual experiences, then you have to ignore the Voice. You can train yourself to disregard what the Voice says. Sometimes it helps to picture a disreputable face that goes with the Voice: You could imagine a snaggletoothed scowling hag speaking—which makes it easier to discount what's being said. The main thing is to recognize when the Voice starts chattering and trying to rob you of great sex. Then close your ears and heart to its lies. In Exodus 20:16, God commands people to not tell lies about others, and that is exactly what the Voice does: It tells lies about you. God is the Author of all truth, and he wants to keep you away from all lies, including the lies you say about yourself.

God's Truth About Sex

Once you've decided to ignore the Voice, move on to the next CWIVES Club strategy for combating the Enemy: Speak to yourself what God says is true about sex, even if you don't yet believe it's the truth. The more you speak the truth in love to yourself, the truer it will feel to you over time. Below are some of God's truths that you can copy for quick reference when the Voice starts ranting.

- *God's Good Women learn how to enjoy sex.* "Let him kiss me with the kisses of his mouth—for your love is more delightful than wine. . . . Take me away with you—let us hurry!" (Song of Songs 1:2, 4).

- *My husband, like most husbands, is captivated by my naked body, no matter my age or weight.* "My darling, I am yours, and you desire me. . . . Just looking at me brings him great pleasure" (Song of Songs 7:10; 8:10 CEV).

- *Making love to my husband is really no trouble. Sex makes a man feel loved.* "You have stolen my heart with one glance of your eyes. . . . How delightful is your love. . . . My desire set me among the royal chariots of my people" (Song of Songs 4:9–10; 6:12).

- *My husband will appreciate and respect me for directly asking for what I want in bed.* "Show me your face, let me hear your voice; for your voice is sweet, and your face is lovely" (Song of Songs 2:14).

- *My husband is my best friend.* "His mouth is sweetness itself; he is altogether lovely. This is my lover, this my friend" (Song of Songs 5:16).

- *My husband and I can fix any sexual problems we have by working together.* "Catch for us the foxes, the little foxes that ruin the vineyards, our vineyards that are in bloom" (Song of Songs 2:15).

- *I can give myself to my husband without reservation, with mind, heart, and body.* "I am my lover's and my lover is mine; he browses among the lilies" (Song of Songs 6:3).

- *God is pleased when my husband and I enjoy one another sexually.* "We rejoice and delight in you; we will praise your love more than wine. . . . Eat, O friends, and drink; drink your fill, O lovers" (Song of Songs 1:4; 5:1).

Club Guidelines

So now you've read the manual and been warned about and equipped to silence Public Enemy Number One, the Voice. All that's left is to go over the CWIVES Club guidelines:

1. No granny gowns unless your husband is out of town. You don't always have to go to bed looking like a lingerie model, but you don't have to look like Ma Ingalls from *Little House on the Prairie* either. Set a goal for yourself of going to bed in something slinky at least once a month. Many women are particularly sexually responsive the week after their period ends, so try scheduling Slinky Night that week.

2. No granny panties even if your husband is out of town. Like your mother said, "Always wear cute panties because you never know when you might be in a car accident and end up in the ER." Okay, maybe your mom actually said to wear clean panties, but cute and clean is even better. And yes, manufacturers

now make attractive underwear and lingerie in plus sizes, so don't use that as an excuse.

3. Be an initiator like the CWIVES Club mascot, the Shulammite (the Beloved from Song of Songs). Don't always wait for your husband to approach you for sex. Christian Nice Girls often settle for boring sex when they could take a page out of the Shulammite's book and plan ahead for fun sex. She prepares to surprise her husband with "every delicacy, both new and old" (Song of Songs 7:13). Women are naturally imaginative and resourceful, so direct some creative juices toward making sex fun rather than expending all your energy on other pursuits. You might find that a regular diet of great sex gives you more energy for other projects.*

*It's a fact: Creative sex can lead to better scrapbooking.

4. Leave the lights on while making love. Not only are you less likely to be accidentally elbowed in the eye, but you can also look your husband in the eyes while making love. That's very intimate. Plus, he enjoys looking at your body, even if you don't. Men are wired that way. They never seem to get bored with seeing a nude woman, so every time he can sneak a peek at your naked body, it's like Christmas morning to him.

5. Don't apologize for your body. Even if you don't like the way you look, don't apologize for or habitually list your perceived physical imperfections.

Here's another way of looking at this common, but counterproductive, habit. One of the biggest mistakes beginners make when entertaining is to apologize for a dish that they believe is flawed. What does this have to do with sex? First, most dinner guests don't even notice culinary mistakes, just like most husbands don't notice their wives' supposed imperfections.

Second, even if they do notice the culinary mistake, most people don't care if something is not perfect—they're just glad that someone else was willing to cook for them. (We're guessing that you can figure out how this applies to husbands and sex.) And third—and this is the most important part—by calling attention to imperfections, you rob others of potential enjoyment, whether in the dining room with food or the bedroom with sex.

6. Don't feign illness or sleep to avoid sex. If you don't want to have sex, then acknowledge your feelings and say, "I don't want to make love right now. How about later today or tomorrow?"* Yes, this might cause your husband disappointment and even anger if you consistently turn him down. But lying is what little girls do to evade going to school or doing chores. Deception has no place in a healthy marriage, particularly in the bedroom, so . . .

*If you have to turn down your spouse's request for sex, give him an alternate time. That way he will see that you are refusing this particular time for sex instead of refusing to have sex forever.

7. Don't fake orgasms. Not even on his birthday. Don't pretend that you have had an orgasm just to be nice. It's not nice to lie to your husband. When you fake orgasms, he assumes that everything he's doing sexually is working well. Men believe "if it ain't broke, don't fix it," so he's unlikely to change his technique if you continue sending the false message that what he's doing now is working great. Meanwhile, you will become secretly resentful toward him because he has no idea how hard you are working to keep up the sexual charade.

Your husband needs to know that occasionally being unable to "get there" happens to most women. He also deserves to know how he could improve his sexual technique so you are

*If you've never been able to orgasm, or frequently cannot orgasm, please consider talking to a therapist, or even a Christian sex therapist if there is one in your area. The American Association of Christian Counselors (www.aacc.net) is a good place to start your therapist search.

more likely to orgasm.* Most husbands want to be excellent lovers, but that will only happen if their wives are willing to speak the truth in love about sex, which takes you into the next guideline. . . .

8. Tell the truth about sexual preferences. Christian Nice Girls prefer to try sexual mental telepathy with their husbands—they think hard about what they wish he would do, push a hand here and there, but won't speak the truth in love while making love.

Your husband is not a mind reader or a nudge reader. He needs clear instructions about how to bring you sexual pleasure, because your pleasure brings him pleasure—that's how God designed men. And God's pivotal principle of speaking the truth in love applies to sexual relationships. So ask yourself: When it comes to sex, am I lying or withholding information about what I want sexually?

Christian Nice Wives feel awkward, anxious, and sometimes even dirty when they think about having a direct conversation about lovemaking preferences. But God created humans with individual preferences, so don't let any negative feelings keep you from speaking the truth. Sometimes it helps to write down what you want to say prior to initiating a sexual discussion. The important thing is to *have* the discussion, and then be patient as you incorporate those preferences into your sex life. And speaking of preferences,

9. Be open to his preferences as well. This doesn't mean that you should be open to sexual activities that degrade you or clearly violate God's Word. Hebrews 13:4 says, "Marriage should be

honored by all, and the marriage bed kept pure, for God will judge the adulterer and all the sexually immoral." Using pornography together is sexually immoral because it invites a third person into your sexual relationship.*

*If pornography has been a part of your sexual relationship, please speak the truth in love to your spouse about its detrimental effect on your spiritual and physical intimacy.

10. Get appropriate treatment for sexual pain, chronic loss of sexual desire, history of sexual abuse, and related problems. There isn't room in this book to adequately address all these issues, but please don't ignore them and the negative effect they can have on your sexual relationship. Talk to your doctor, talk to a therapist, read some books—just get the help you need and deserve. And remember that your best source of help comes when you . . .

11. Pray to God about your sexuality. Christian Nice Wives think it's weird to pray about that, but remember, sex was God's idea. He invented it. You may feel awkward when you first talk to God about sex. But he wants to help when it's 11:00 p.m. and you're tired and your husband wants to make love. So while you are brushing your teeth, pray for extra energy and for your body to thrill to your husband's touch. God specializes in bringing dead things back to life, so you might be pleasantly surprised at what comes alive. CWIVES Club members keep their sexual relationship near the top of their prayer list.

12. One final guideline: Don't remain willfully ignorant of your husband's legitimate need for regular sex with an active, interested partner. You've heard the woman's perspective for most of this chapter, but here is your husband's perspective à la Paul: Biblically, a man or woman can have their other human needs met by other people. As a man, I can have my clothes

ironed at the cleaners. I can have my meals cooked down the street night after night. I can receive companionship at work and emotional support from my sister and close guy friends and my pastor. But what I cannot, biblically, receive from any other woman in my life is sex. My wife holds the key, which is both a blessing and a curse. As I hear too many times during conferences, when wives withhold sex from their husbands, men naturally become very resentful—especially Christian men who waited until marriage to have sex.

Sex for men is like looking at two fruit trees. One says Marriage Tree and the other says Adultery Tree. I am hungry and I want to eat. I **need** to eat, and I want to eat from the Marriage Tree, I really do, but the Marriage Tree just makes it too darn hard to pick its fruit sometimes. The Adultery Tree is hard to get to as well, and I don't want to go that direction, which helps me resist it. But when I'm starving—well, the Adultery Tree is just so tempting. And eventually the Adultery Tree clears away the usual brambles and creates a very easy path, full of compliments and even exuberance. None of this excuses unfaithfulness, and I'm not trying to blame wives for their husbands' adultery. This is simply an explanation of the powerful, conflicting forces that war inside of men, particularly when their wives withhold sex.

You're still breathing, so you must have made it through the sex chapter without dying of embarrassment. If you are ready to become a full-fledged member of the Christian Wives Initiating, Valuing, and Enjoying Sex Club, cross your heart and say:

I promise to uphold the hallowed CWIVES Club traditions of cute panties, Slinky Night, leaving the lights on, and taking the initiative. I will not fake orgasms, pretend to be asleep, or apologize for my body. I pledge to speak the truth about my sexual preferences, be open to my husband's preferences, be aware of his need for sex on a regular basis, get treatment for sexual issues, and frequently talk with God about my sexual relationship.

Welcome to the Club!*

For more fun and helpful information on understanding and enhancing your sexuality as a Christian wife, check out www.cwives.com.

CNG Nicole

The tantalizing smell of coffee tickles Nicole's nose. She opens one eye and sees David sitting on the edge of their bed, smiling.

"Good morning. I brought you a cup of coffee."

Pushing herself up into a sitting position, Nicole stretches.

"Thank you. What time is it?"

"It's almost nine. You must have been really tired." David winks. "I was pretty wiped out this morning too after last night."

Nicole feels a light blush heating her cheeks, then laughs softly. "I can't believe I'm actually blushing. We've been married for years."

"Yeah, but last night was like a honeymoon. What got into you? I'm not complaining, mind you—I'm just curious."

"I don't know . . . I guess it's this book I've been reading. It's called *No More Christian Nice Girl.*"

David smiles a wide, Cheshire cat grin. "Honey, after last night, you are definitely not a nice girl. You are all woman."

"David!" Nicole throws a pillow at him, laughing. "You make me sound like some kind of wild woman!"

"Nothing wrong with wild. And when you're swinging from the chandelier, that's considered wild."

"We were not swinging from the chandelier! We don't even own a chandelier."

161

David laughs, sets down Nicole's coffee mug, and heads for the bedroom door. "Okay, then swinging from the ceiling fan."

He pauses, turning back toward Nicole. "Last night really was amazing. I'm a lucky man."

Nicole smiles lazily, nestling back down under the bedcovers. "You sure are. Go make me an omelet, and maybe you'll get lucky again after breakfast."

Study Questions

1. When it comes to sex, do you feel more like a little girl or an adult woman? What could you do to grow in the area of sexuality?

2. Where is sex on your priority list? If sex is way down on your list, what could you do to make it a higher priority? In what ways might your marriage benefit if you prioritized sex?

3. Prior to reading this chapter and Song of Songs, what did you believe was God's opinion of sex? Has your belief changed?

4. The Voice, or the internal critic, lies to and taunts women about their bodies and their sexuality. What sort of critical messages have you heard and possibly believed?

5. How do you react when those critical thoughts surface? Has this affected your sexual relationship? Share with your group any tips you have for silencing the Voice.

6. Review the list of God's truths about sex. Which of these do you need to start believing? How would your sexual relationship change if you believed and acted upon these truths?

7. Review the CWIVES Club guidelines. Which of these would you be willing to implement first? What obstacles could prevent you from following through? What could you do to overcome these obstacles? Ask your group for suggestions if needed.

8. What was your reaction to reading a husband's perspective (à la Paul) on married sex? Do you need to discuss this topic with your husband?

Bonus Bible Study Question: Read Genesis 2:24–25; Song of Songs 6:3; 7:10; 8:10; and 1 Corinthians 7:3–5. Looking at these passages, how does God want husbands and wives to see their bodies in relation to each other? How does this godly perspective bless couples?

CHAPTER NINE

Work: How Nice Cripples Your Career

If you are considering skipping this chapter because you don't work outside the home, don't touch that dial! There's helpful information here for all women who have an occupation, so whether you are occupied with paid work (doctor, hair stylist, sales, restaurant industry, teacher, etc.) or unpaid work (PTA volunteer, committee member, small group leader, etc.), keep reading. We'll show you how to work and compete more successfully in a variety of settings.

Did somebody just mention the word *compete*? That's not always an easy word for Christian Nice Girls to hear. In fact, words like *competition* can trip up a CNG quicker than four-inch stilettos.

Before revealing what makes CNGs, in particular, stumble at work, let's look quickly at the factors that make navigating the work world challenging for most women. In chapter 2, you saw how God divinely created women's brains and hormones for connections with other people. All women bring with them to work their affinity for relationships. Females tend to see the workplace as a network of connections where friendships are established as people cooperate to produce work. Nothing is wrong with that viewpoint until you realize that, by and large, the work world was created by men—males who tend to see the workplace as a field for competition where winners and losers emerge as people compete *and* cooperate to produce work.

And while more girls are now getting team and leadership experiences from sports and extracurricular activities, many women still feel more uncomfortable than men do with open competition and direct leadership. Oh, and the pressure women experience from the Nice Girl Culture to be unrelentingly sweet, compliant, and cooperative doesn't let up at work or in volunteer settings either.

All women experience these challenges at work, but CNGs carry the extra burden of a strong need for approval. Yes, they want to be successful, but their people-pleasing part wants something else: to make everyone happy. Their conflicting desires of "I want to succeed" and "I want to be liked by everyone" drag them in two different directions. Given this relentless tug-of-war, it's no surprise that work environments, paid and volunteer, often exhaust CNGs and leave them feeling confused, taken advantage of, and passed over. They want to perform well, but they also fear being socially rejected if they perform *too* well. What's a girl to do?

It's Hard to Get by Just Upon a Smile, Girl

Well, the first thing to do is to acknowledge that competition isn't a bad thing; in fact, it can be a very positive force that, when handled well, helps women grow as they realize that they are stronger and more capable than they ever imagined. God can use competition to help you mature and become more like the 360-degree Jesus.

We hope you agree that competition can be a good thing, because, guess what? All work involves competition because jobs are limited resources—there's only so much to go around. Even if you are cleaning septic tanks for a living, there is someone else who would like to have your job, so you are competing against other applicants to be the person hired.* You also compete for consumers because you will only have a job if people choose to come to your particular store, office, bank, restaurant, hospital, school, etc., and "buy" what you produce. Because these situations require competing against unknown people (e.g., the other job applicants, professionals in other offices offering the same services, etc.), most Christian Nice Girls can tolerate this type

*Okay, so maybe there isn't a long line of people wanting to be septic tank cleaners, but you get our point.

of remote competition. It's easier for them to personally succeed when they can't see the whites of their competitors' eyes. The trouble starts when CNGs have to compete against people they know: their co-workers.

If you are thinking, *My co-workers and I don't compete, we are one big happy family,* brace yourself for a cold splash of reality. You can establish friendships in the workplace, but work at times will be a game with winners and losers. If you don't realize that, you are being naïve, and you are going to get hurt and taken advantage of. Now don't get paranoid—you don't have to become cutthroat and sabotage people in order to succeed, but you do need to be informed and wise in the ways of the work world. Jesus wanted his disciples to be savvy in their work, which is why he told them in Matthew 10:16: "I am sending you out like sheep among wolves. Therefore be as shrewd as snakes and as innocent as doves."

Sadly, Christian Nice Girls often realize far too late that they have squandered immeasurable time and energy at work worshiping at the altar of other people's approval instead of investing their resources in advancing their careers. For years, they watch with confusion and resentment as co-workers (whom they judge to be far less nice and thus less deserving) receive "their" promotions, raises, and accolades, never realizing that the 360-degree Jesus could provide a much-needed, courageous, truth-speaking example of how to succeed at work by being both gracious and firm.

You're Fired!

In order to become the savvy, shrewd woman Jesus had in mind, you may need to practice this infamous phrase: "You're fired!" Don't worry, you won't be passing out pink slips to people—what needs firing are the behaviors that are holding you back from being God's Good Working Woman.

Here are some passive, self-defeating workplace behaviors that limit the success of CNGs. Which of these do you need to fire?

Remaining silent in meetings, particularly mixed meetings. The Nice Girl Culture teaches females not to interrupt other people and to wait to speak until called upon. Unfortunately, these are little-girl behaviors that do not translate into the modern world of work. Women tend to be quieter in meetings where men are present. When they let the men do most of the talking, the men will naturally get most of the credit. Because men interrupt more often than women do, you need to learn to handle being interrupted rather than allowing the interruption to silence you. Think of an interruption not as a period in a sentence that ends a thought, but as a comma that merely pauses the thought. Your job is to complete the rest of the sentence.

Here's an example:

Susan: "Our Web site isn't bringing in as much traffic as we hoped. I suggest that we—"

Bill: "Our Web site is boring, that's the problem. And it's hard to navigate. We should blah, blah, blah. . . ."

Susan: (sits in silence, fuming)

Or Susan could interrupt Bill so that she could finish her thought after the comma created by Bill.

Susan: "Our Web site isn't bringing in as much traffic as we hoped. I suggest that we—"

Bill: "Our Web site is boring, that's the problem. And it's hard to navigate. We should—"

Susan: "Excuse me, Bill, I wasn't through speaking. Because our Web site isn't bringing in as much traffic as we want, I suggest we consult with another Web hosting company and get their perspective. Now Bill, I heard your concern about our Web site. Specifically, how is our Web site boring, and what would you do to fix this perceived problem?"

Contrary to what the Nice Girl Culture teaches, Susan is not being rude by interrupting Bill. She had the floor, he took the floor by interrupting her, and now she is simply taking back what was hers, that is, the floor. When you are speaking in a meeting, it's helpful to imagine that you are holding an actual piece of the floor, and that whoever interrupts you has snatched the floor from your hands. This imagery may help you recognize what just happened, and that you need to graciously but firmly take the floor back.

Also, from a boss's perspective, your failure to speak up in such a meeting can be irritating. If the supervisor running the meeting is a true leader who wants to hear several perspectives before making an informed decision, that person will want to hear from everyone—including you, the Christian Nice Girl. If you continue to be Switzerland—neutral on everything important—you will actually frustrate your boss by not being honest about your opinions, because sharing your opinion is part of your job. You get paid to speak up.

You may also frustrate your boss if she or he knows, from past experience, that the "nice" women in the office/restaurant/school/store/hospital will be among the first to have "the meeting after the meeting." That's when they finally speak up, only to mainly criticize what others said and decided. They had their chance to effect change, but they refused to participate and instead chose to feed the Nice Girl Culture of unproductive cattiness.

Rescuing incompetent co-workers by doing their work.[1] Most people grow up watching mothers pick up after their children, finish the last of the dishes, etc. Women like to help, and it is hard to stop this rescuing behavior in the workplace. But it's a big mistake to rescue incompetent co-workers by doing their work for them. Everyone needs a helping hand now and again, but there is a difference between giving someone a helping hand and enabling them to be a perpetual slacker. Look around and ask yourself: Is anyone else helping this person out? Am I the only one who seems to think this person needs rescuing? Continuing to rescue someone in the workplace is usually a sign that the person is in the wrong position and needs to evolve as an employee. Unless the other person is willing to change for the better, your efforts are prolonging the inevitable termination and wasting your time and energy. Follow the example of the 360-degree Jesus and point out where they need to improve their performance without shaming them as a person.

Trying too hard not to be offensive.[2] If your primary goal is to be well-liked at work, you will probably end up trying too hard not to offend anyone, ever. But the nature of competition, of supply and demand, requires change, and change inevitably makes waves. It's built into the system.

CNGs believe that creating waves is offensive, and that only "bad" people make waves at work. Yes, it's true that there are people who are unwilling to control their tongues and inordinate ambitions, and who love to create tumultuous waves of useless drama. But God's Good Working Women make the right kind of waves, the kind that benefit themselves and their organizations, even if those waves bring changes that don't feel comfortable at first. Remember: A wave-free existence is the state of a person's life just before drowning. So ask yourself: Do I occasionally make waves at work, and what effect do my waves have?

And keep in mind that Jesus was offensive at times, even to his co-workers, the disciples. If you aren't offending someone occasionally by speaking the truth at work, you are likely too wishy-washy and are coming across as lacking depth or backbone. We aren't suggesting that you should start telling offensive jokes or doing things that would be immoral, illegal, or unethical. Just be willing to voice your opinion without backing away, apologizing, or otherwise negating what you've said.

CNGs who won't say no for fear of offending someone will be taken advantage of and possibly even led into sin by spiritually immature colleagues and clients. For example, you might be serving on a church's building committee and seeking sealed construction bids when a fellow church member asks you to reveal the secret bid amounts so that his construction company can submit the winning lowest bid. When someone asks God's Good Working Women to bend the rules like this, they say no, without apology, even if the other person gets offended and threatens to make a stink. The same applies when you are working with customers and they try to get you to ignore company policies or negotiate a shady deal. Just keep saying no, graciously but firmly, even if they threaten to take their business elsewhere.

I (Paul) have worked many years for a chamber of commerce that is not afraid to take strong political stances on behalf of business. It's a big part of the purpose of the organization, and it has strained some of my friendships. If my organization shied away from political battles in order to retain popularity, it would not be serving its members well. And if this fact caused me to back down, then I wouldn't be fulfilling the organization's mission. I wouldn't be serving the membership who need me to fight on their behalf. Chances are you have similar decisions to make in your job.

Polling prior to making any decision.[3] Although Proverbs says that there is wisdom found in many counselors, CNGs tend to ask far too many people for their opinion prior to making a decision. Repeatedly seeking wise counsel is a good thing; repeatedly seeking stamps of approval is a sad thing. Why do CNGs go from person to person asking, "Do you think I should do this?" Answer: Because they want other people's approval and/or their permission. This is little-girl behavior, and it makes women look uncertain, weak, and incompetent at work. If you could benefit from someone's wise counsel about a decision, rather than approach them with "What do you think I should do?" try saying, "I've got a situation I'd like to run past you and get your input on." That way you are consulting with someone, adult to adult. If the person you're talking with is above you in management, this consultative approach could also help you get potential "buy in" with your idea before you unfold it.

Sharing too much personal information in an effort to be well-liked.[4] Women bond by sharing the intimate details of their lives, so they naturally tend to carry this behavior over into work settings. Because of their strong need for approval, Christian Nice Girls share more than is necessary or wise to connect with others. This can come back to haunt them when it's time for promotions and raises. If you have shared with your co-workers intimate details about your marital problems, wayward children, financial difficulties, new job searches, etc., and then are promoted over those same co-workers, you may be unpleasantly surprised at how those secrets are divulged and discussed by the very people you now have to supervise. Or your potential raise may be canceled when your co-worker reveals to your boss that you are considering taking a new job.

In the workplace, it's fine to share some basic personal information, such as your marital status or whether you have children, but note how men often don't share this kind of information right away. They talk about their qualifications for work, such as college degrees or specialized training, and are friendly toward one another without divulging intimate secrets. This is shrewd behavior that God's Good Working Women should consider as well, particularly if there is any chance that they might one day be in a supervisory position over their fellow bank tellers / salespeople / administrative assistants / attorneys, etc. Remember: (1) you are there to work and produce, not to find your best friend or to endear yourself to the whole workplace; and (2) the 360-degree Jesus didn't share too much personal information and rarely answered a question directly.

Either calling too much attention to or covering up mistakes you make. This is where fear and perfectionistic worry ambush a CNG—when she makes one error and multiplies it into a much bigger one by either releasing a deluge of information about her mistakes or hiding / denying any wrongdoing like a little girl would. Her anxiety over not doing things perfectly prevents her from doing the most important thing: learning from her mistakes and making amends if possible. Your boss and colleagues know that adults make errors. They want you to learn from your mistakes—not ruminate upon or hide them—so that you can get back to being productive.

Making knee-jerk decisions in order to relieve anxiety. When CNGs fear conflict and the tension that accompanies unresolved matters, they can be too quick to provide a short-term "answer" to a problem that may cause them long-term difficulties. Cunning people in the workplace know this and will use it against you. Your hasty reflex decision is their gain, so they will sometimes spring information on you *deliberately*. For example, manipulative co-workers who are aware of certain organizational developments may withhold this information until it is to their advantage to share it. They will wait until the last moment to reveal this crucial information and then press CNGs for an immediate (and unwise) decision.

Case in point: I (Paul) once had a co-worker who asked me to create a long list of contacts for her, a list that she actually needed weeks earlier (a fact she kept to herself). She waited until right before her planned vacation to ask for the contact list and then said that she didn't have time to call everyone and asked me to contact them instead. This way she could make it look like she wanted to do her job but just couldn't due to her vacation. And she could try to portray me as not being a team player if I made the decision not to make the phone calls on her behalf (calls I was ill-equipped to make). If I had responded with a knee-jerk yes, I would have been in the dangerous position of doing another's work without the knowledge of how to do it successfully.

To defend yourself against this type of "user" in the workplace, use this handy comeback when you are pressed for an immediate decision: "I'll have to get back to you on that." This response will give you time to think and pray about your decision, seek more information or wise counsel if necessary, and formulate a professional answer.

Turning down promotions because of fear of cattiness. Unfortunately, when a woman is promoted, she may experience cattiness from her female co-workers who are now her subordinates and who are uncomfortable with her change in power and status. It can feel like middle school all over again as she is gossiped about, sabotaged, or shunned. Some CNGs with a high need to keep everyone happy may find this conflict and rejection so painful that they refuse all promotions or step down as supervisors, severely limiting their professional advancement. God's Good Working Women accept the promotions they earn but manage their power and relationships carefully (more on this later in the chapter).

Refusing to confront subordinates about problems. Because of their strong need to be well-liked and their fear of conflict, CNGs who manage other people are regularly taken advantage of by their subordinates. Routine tardiness, chronic absenteeism, unprofessional behavior with customers, lackadaisical job performance, bad attitudes, unreasonable requests for time off—these often go unchallenged by anxious, pushover CNG managers who avoid necessary confrontations. Learn from the example of Jesus managing his people. In John 12, he directly confronted the indignant Judas when he gave Mary of Bethany a hard time about anointing Jesus with an expensive perfume. In Mark 10, when James and John made an unreasonable request to be honored above the other disciples, Jesus told them flat-out that they didn't know what they were asking for and refused their request. He didn't let fear of conflict or the fear of being talked about negatively keep him from managing his people effectively.

You're Hired!

Now that you've seen which behaviors deserve a pink slip, take a look at these prospective applicants for hire. All of these behaviors will help you become a more productive, truthful woman of integrity in work or volunteer settings. Pick out the one behavior that seems easiest to implement at your current workplace. Successfully practicing this new skill will give you more confidence and courage to tackle the others on the list:

Making more independent decisions and then taking responsibility for the consequences—good or bad. This means that you share the praise or blame, accurately and honestly, with others. So you accept praise without false humility (pretending that you contributed nothing meaningful is really a lie in disguise) or putting your contributions down ("Thanks, but my part was lame compared to everyone else's contribution."). This also means that if your decision failed because someone else didn't do their job, you are free to point out this contributing factor if you are asked to provide an explanation. Just be sure to speak the truth **in love** so you don't end up scapegoating someone else.

Taking more calculated risks instead of always playing it safe. Your life will blossom or shrivel based upon the courage you have to act. Take smart risks that will require you to confront some fear in your life such as accepting more responsibility or applying for a new position. Go beyond your job description occasionally to tackle a persistent issue or opportunity. When your God-given creativity and intuition lead you to recognize problems and solutions that no one else has seen yet, don't play it safe and hide these ideas in a dark closet. Take a risk—get those ideas out, give them some air, and see what develops.

Trusting your intuition more. If something doesn't seem right to you, if it raises red flags, then listen to your gut. Don't listen to the anxious, people-pleasing part that wants you to ignore your intuition and just act nice. Ask for more information so you can make a wiser, more informed decision. God gave you a brain and, if you are a Christian, the Holy Spirit—both of which can help you discern truth from fiction. Trust these gifts.

Setting appropriate boundaries on your time, treasure, and talent. For CNGs, this almost always means that you should value all three more, not less. God gave you the three Ts because he wants your life to matter, and he expects you to use them wisely. This means guarding your time at work and away from work so that you can be productive in all areas of life. For example, if co-workers are monopolizing your work time talking about their personal problems, it's your job to set a boundary with them. You can say, "I know that this personal problem is really weighing you down, but I have to get back to work now." If a chronic time-monopolizer calls at work and asks in a sad voice, "Have you got a minute to talk?" God's Good Working Women know that the "minute" will likely turn into thirty minutes, and so they respond with, "No, I'm sorry, I don't. I'm right in the middle of something." That's not rude, that's the truth. You are right in the middle of working.

Here are some more examples: If your boss repeatedly expects you to take work home at night or on the weekends, then it's your job to set a boundary around your home time and say, "My work load is too much for me to accomplish during regular working hours. Let's look at my job responsibilities and see which of these may need to be postponed or given to someone else to do." Or if you are talented in a particular area, let's say graphic design, and your co-workers or boss repeatedly request that you use these talents for non-work-related projects (like designing their family Christmas letter), it's your job to set boundaries around your talent by saying, "I'm appreciative that you like my design work, but I'm not able to do personal projects for people on company time," or, "Between the demands of work and home, I don't have any extra time to do personal projects for people."

Adapting to the other person's communication style.[5] There are two styles of communication: direct (tell it like it is) and indirect (hint, make suggestions, or ask questions about problems). For example, if a conference room is overheated, a direct communicator (usually male) will say, "It's too hot in here," while an indirect communicator (usually female) will ask, "Is anyone getting too warm in here?" Both styles have value, so if you want to work successfully with both sexes, you need to learn to adapt to the communication style of whomever you are speaking with. This flexibility is hard for CNGs. They worry that directly "telling it like it is" will offend someone. As a result, CNGs stick with the indirect style, which is then heard as uncertainty and insecurity by most men—the same men who may decide who gets promoted and who gets passed over because she always sounds unsure to them.

God's Good Working Women flex to the other person's communication style. So if you are talking with a direct person, present your ideas in a straightforward, logical manner, but if you are speaking with an indirect person, use a more feeling-oriented, participatory style. For example, if you are managing a retail store, you could say to your direct communicators, "There is a problem with these clothing displays. Please look at this photograph from headquarters and make the display match the photo." Most men speak this way and will respond well to this kind of direct management from either a male or female supervisor.

However, because of the influence of the Nice Girl Culture and the high value women place on connections, women typically will resent a female supervisor using that kind of direct communication with them. It feels too abrupt, like "she's just throwing her weight around." So your indirect communicators will respond better to "Hmmm . . . something doesn't feel right with these clothing displays. We're supposed to make the display match this photo. What do you think we should change to make them match up?" This type of participatory, process-oriented communication will make female employees feel included in the decision-making process and will reaffirm that you value your connection to them. You will also reduce the chances of catty behavior erupting. We have encouraged directly speaking the truth in love throughout this book, but when you find yourself having to tell other women what to do, your savviest choice is often to adopt their indirect style. That's not being manipulative or weak. That's being smart.

Managing your chips effectively. It's not your potato chip intake we are referring to here. As Pat Heim, Susan Murphy, and Susan Golant explain in their book *In the Company of Women*, everyone "is endowed with a certain number of chips of power—positive attributes or actions—that we constantly exchange with others."[6] God's Good Working Women (and men) use these chips to manage their power and relationships effectively. Some examples of chips that you can give and/or receive at work include:

- Encouraging words, including authentic praise and the specifics of what was done well.
- Supportive words, including genuine empathy for difficult situations.
- Small talk, including asking personal (but not private) questions about family members, pets, recent personal events, etc.
- Sincere compliments on clothing, professional skills, or business sense.
- Sharing personal (but not private) details from your own life.
- Asking for the other person's input, opinion, advice.
- Little gifts, like a cup of coffee.
- Thank-you notes.
- Raises and promotions.
- Providing opportunities to: be creative, earn bonuses, work with upper management or key clients, make presentations to supervisors or important customers.
- Mentoring or providing career planning and assistance.[7]

Heim, Murphy, and Golant add that in the workplace "everyone with whom you interact keeps a chip bankbook on you. All day long you are gaining and losing chips with your direct reports, peers, and higher-ups. They know where you stand with them at any given moment, and you know where they stand with you. . . . One of the

most important rules . . . is that *we always make it equal in the end*—
that is, if someone tries to take away our chips, we will find a way
to even the score."[8]

For example, let's say you teach second grade and share a teacher's
aide with three other teachers. Lately you haven't had time to chat
with her for a few minutes each day, and you also haven't asked to see
the photos from her daughter's recent wedding. Don't be surprised if
your papers are now the last to be graded by the teacher's aide. Why?
Because she's making the chips equal in the end.

To manage your relationships in a savvy manner at work, find
out who values what kind of chips, and then stockpile those particular types of chips with others who can help you be more productive
and successful. Female co-workers tend to prize "chitchat" chips,
but you could end up costing yourself chips if you chat too much
with male (or female) co-workers who might not value small talk.
Carefully observe your colleagues to discover their individual chip
preferences. Be sure to include the janitor. Your boss may control
the promotions, but when the heat isn't working in your office,
you'll be glad that you have a chip surplus with the maintenance
crew.

If this sounds like a game, that's because it is. Remember how
we said earlier that work at times will be a game with winners and
losers? CNGs end up losing at the game of work in part because
they expend their energy giving chips to the spiritually immature in
their work or volunteer setting instead of learning to be savvy chip
managers like God's Good Working Women.

After working so hard doing all this firing and hiring, you deserve
some time off! Hey, how about a road trip? Grab your keys, girlfriend—
we have one more chapter left, and it starts with you in the driver's
seat.

CNG Nicole

Stepping into Nicole's office, Mike asks, "Have you got a minute?"

"Sure, what's up?"

Mike smiles sheepishly. "I've double-booked myself. I agreed to get these budget figures to Human Resources by three, but I forgot a personal matter that I have to take care of this afternoon. Could you finish running the numbers, e-mail them, and then call HR to answer questions? Won't take you more than an hour."

Nicole checks her schedule and thinks, *Yeah, right, that hour is probably more like all afternoon.* "I don't know, Mike. I'm pretty swamped right now. Is the personal matter something you can't reschedule?"

"It's really important, or I wouldn't ask. Thanks for helping me out." Mike moves toward the door.

"Hang on. I didn't agree to do this yet. Let me think about it, and I'll get back to you."

Looking surprised, Mike sputters, "Well, okay. That'd be great."

After he leaves, Nicole ponders the situation. *Mike hasn't been particularly trustworthy in the past. My intuition is telling me something, so I should do a little checking before I agree to this.*

Deciding to ask Mike for more information, Nicole walks toward his office, turning the corner just in time to hear a sales representative's departing words.

" . . . glad you could clear your afternoon, Mike. See you on the tee box at noon."

Nicole's jaw drops. *I am not doing my work plus Mike's work so that he can go play golf. If he had a doctor's appointment or his child was in a school program, that would be different, but golf? I don't think so.*

Walking the rest of the way to Mike's door, Nicole leans her head in his office.

"Hey, Mike, I'm not going to be able to cover for you this afternoon."

"Well, why not?" huffs Mike.

"There's not room in my day to add in one more project."

"Really?" Mike asks. "What do you have going on?"

Nicole considers Mike's entrapping question. *I used to think I owed people complete access to my life. I'm not making that mistake anymore.* "My schedule is my schedule, Mike, just like your schedule is your schedule. Sometimes I can change it, and sometimes I can't."

Mike sighs. "Nicole, I was really counting on you to help me out."

With a slight smile, Nicole says, "Yes, I know helping you out has been par for the course for me, but it's not going to work out today. I'll see you later."

Smiling as she walks back into her office, Nicole mimics swinging a golf club. *And that's how you avoid the Nice Girl sand trap!*

Study Questions

1. When you are in a competitive situation, how do you feel? How do you react?

2. Are you satisfied with your success in your workplace or volunteer setting? If not, what factors are contributing to your dissatisfaction or lack of success?

3. Do you ever feel conflicted over wanting to be assertive and firm at work, yet at the same time wanting to be caring and warm? What situations or people bring out this conflict most often for you?

4. Do you have an example of a woman who is both gracious and firm in your workplace or volunteer/ministry setting? If not,

is there a woman in the popular media who could serve as an example? Discuss with your group how she is able to strike this essential balance.

5. How do you typically behave in meetings? Do you need to share your opinions more often at work? If so, when would be a good time for you to practice this skill?

6. How do you think women can retain their femininity at work while also not getting run over?

7. Share with your group if any of the following Christian Nice Girl behaviors are impeding your success at work or in volunteer settings: rescuing incompetent workers by doing their work, trying too hard not to be offensive, polling prior to making decisions, calling too much attention to or covering up mistakes, making knee-jerk decisions, turning down promotions, or refusing to confront subordinates. What could you do differently in those situations?

8. Have you ever shared too much personal information with someone and later regretted it? What advice would you give Christian women who want to succeed in their workplaces but also want to develop good relationships with co-workers?

9. Jesus rarely answered a question directly, yet many Christian women think that they owe others in the workplace complete candor. What does this tell you about how Jesus behaved and how many Christians think they are expected to behave?

10. Share with your group which of the following savvy behaviors would be the easiest for you to begin implementing at work:

making more independent decisions, taking more calculated risks, trusting your intuition more, setting appropriate boundaries, adapting to the other person's communication style, managing your chips effectively. What steps do you need to take to implement that behavior? What obstacles could get in your way and what will you do to overcome those obstacles? Ask your group for suggestions if needed.

Bonus Bible Study Question: Read Numbers 27:1–11. What helpful business lessons can you learn from the way Zelophehad's daughters handled their legal situation?

CHAPTER TEN

The Journey From Christian Nice Girl to God's Good Woman

Doesn't it feel great to reach the last chapter of a book? Your laundry may be piled waist-deep by now, but learning how to be God's Good Woman is far more important than matching up socks (besides, clean clothes are highly overrated). It's challenging to look at what's really behind the plastic, passive niceness that passes for Christianity in many women's lives, and then to boldly choose to be authentic instead. But as you've seen, that's the only way to truly experience the abundant life Jesus promises in John 10:10.

Although this book is coming to an end, your journey from Christian Nice Girl to God's Good Woman continues. And guess who is driving? Yes, that's you in the driver's seat, looking smart with your sunglasses perched on your head. You are ready to roll, but before you drive out of sight, here are a few reminders for the road.

Reminders for the Road

1. Know where you are headed. For all of God's Good Women, the destination is the same: being like Jesus Christ, in all his glorious 360 degrees of salty sweetness. In order to keep this destination clear in your mind, you will have to get know Jesus better and better so that you recognize who he is and where he is at work. Prayer and getting involved in a Bible study are great ways to get to know Jesus better, along with regularly worshiping and fellowshiping with other believers. Just make sure that you are doing these spiritual disciplines to get to know Jesus better, not to earn God's approval or love. God already loves you—it's a done deal—so you don't have to earn his love.

Be aware that when you reveal your destination to others, they may not like where you are headed. Some will even point you in a different direction, back toward where you came from. These people think they are giving you helpful directions, but in reality, they want you to go back to being a Christian Nice Girl because God's Good Women make them uncomfortable. Just thank them for their interest and ignore their directions that will take you to the back side of nowhere, also known as Nice Girl City.

2. Pack only what you will need. God's Good Women don't want to travel with too much junk in their trunk, so pack the essentials and leave the rest behind. Your first essential: courage, which means you'll have to leave behind the cowardice discussed in chapter 3.

Courage grows when you act in spite of your fear. You actually can't be courageous unless you feel fear. So to grow your courage, be aware of your anxiety and then discipline yourself to listen to the Holy Spirit saying, "Something is at stake here that is more important than your fear." A courageous spirit is a mark of the Holy Spirit: "For God did not give us a spirit of timidity, but a spirit of power, of love and of self-discipline" (2 Timothy 1:7). Power and strength are nearly synonymous with courage, so God actually gives you a spirit of courageous strength.

Here are some Scriptures that are worth packing if you could use a whole trunk full of courage:

Be strong and very courageous.

Joshua 1:7

So do not fear, for I am with you; do not be dismayed, for I am your God. I will strengthen you and help you; I will uphold you with my righteous right hand.

Isaiah 41:10

Be on guard. Stand firm in the faith. Be courageous. Be strong.

1 Corinthians 16:13 NLT

To handle your newfound courage well, you need to be aware of rashness, or stupid courage. Rashness is when you do something daring but dumb—you acted without wisdom. The Bible says to do the right thing when it's within your power to act. Sometimes you won't have the power to change a situation for the better. For example, in some extended family situations, it might be best not to speak the truth in love. When your motive for holding your tongue or not acting is based on wisdom, not fear, you are choosing an intelligent behavior called "active passivity," such as when you choose to give an armed robber your purse instead of foolishly refusing.

In addition to courage, you'll need to pack a sense of humor. You need to be able to laugh at yourself because you are going to make some mistakes along the way, some of which will be doozies. However, don't hide them, because often your best life lessons will come out of your biggest mistakes, and your silliest mistakes will produce your funniest stories.

Packing that essential sense of humor means you will have to leave behind your need to appear perfect, and instead be appropriately transparent with others. It takes practice to find that balance between hiding everything and sharing too much, so be patient with yourself as you practice healthy transparency. Occasionally, ask a trusted friend for feedback on whether you are hiding too much or sharing too much so that you can monitor your progress.

3. Choose your travel companions wisely. God's Good Women rarely journey alone for long, so pick carefully who gets to ride next to you. Spiritually mature people should be occupying your passenger seat because when the driver gets lost, who does the navigating? That's right, it's the person riding shotgun. You want people nearby who can read a map—in particular, people who read and understand the Map, also known as the Bible. You want people who know the Way. If they don't, they won't recognize your destination, the 360-degree Jesus, so they are likely to direct you right back to Nice Girl City. And who wants to go back to that saccharine-sweet place?

As we discussed in chapter 5, it takes time to find and cultivate relationships with spiritually mature people, but they are out there. Look for women who speak the truth in love, laugh easily at themselves, talk openly about their faith, are trailblazers in their own lives, and can both celebrate and cry with other people. You are looking for Balcony Women: women who will cheer you on and give you courage and confidence by hanging over the railing of your life, declaring, "I believe in you! You can do it!"

My (Paul's) wife, Sandy, knows how crucial Balcony Women are to God's Good Women. She created what she calls "Balcony Girls," a group of around eight elementary-school-aged girls who get together once a month to do a craft, eat some fun food, and learn valuable life lessons. Balcony Girls groups help girls form a group of friends at school who can help them withstand damaging peer pressure or bullying. They can learn early in life how to grow into Balcony Women, the kind of women who genuinely love and support each other.[1] Your journey will be much more energizing and fun if you have a Balcony Woman buckled in your passenger seat.

Now, sometimes you can't avoid traveling with "getting there" people in your backseat, perhaps because God has clearly told you to let them ride with you for a while or perhaps because . . . well . . . you gave birth to them or are related to them in some way. So there they are—occasionally providing you with spiritually stimulating conversation and occasionally fussing and whining like kids stuck in a station wagon backseat. "Are we there yet? When are you going to stop changing? I liked you better when you were nicer. I need you: to help me right this minute, to do my work, to lend me money, to listen to my endless complaining, and (of course) I need to go to the bathroom."

If pulling over and putting them all out on the side of the road is not a legal option in your state, then you'll have to set boundaries on what is and what is not acceptable behavior in your car, that is, your life. You have to set limits with "getting there" people, or they will tend to take increasingly large amounts of the energy, time, money, and talent God gave you to accomplish his purposes.

If some of them are backseat drivers who enjoy criticizing your every move, feel free to "turn up the radio" to drown out their discouraging words. This means that you distract yourself from truly hearing and taking in their unhelpful criticisms, perhaps by determinedly changing the subject (like Nicole did with her mother in chapter 5) or by reciting scriptural truths or singing praise songs in your mind to counteract their negative words. It's almost like you become the limo driver behind the glass partition—you can lower the glass when you want to listen and raise it when you don't. You'll see their lips moving, but you won't really hear them.

Beware of picking up hitchhikers. They are the "spiritually

immature," the shark-like Mr. Wrongs, the selfish users of this world who want to flag you down and hijack your life. They will do everything in their power to convince or coerce you to go back to Nice Girl City. Why? Because you were much easier to manipulate back there.

4. Don't turn back just because difficulties occur. It's impossible to drive for any length of time and not run into road hazards. The same is true for your journey to becoming God's Good Woman. You are going to encounter difficulties. Expect construction delays because major changes are happening—**you** are under construction, becoming more like the 360-degree Jesus. You can expect other drivers to frown and complain if your new construction causes them even a moment of inconvenience. And you'll get some rubbernecking too. Some drivers like to slow down and stare as other people work hard, so try not to let the occasional shocked look or swiveled head keep you from your work.

Your road hazards may be sudden, jarring potholes that rattle your spirit, like unkind words or deeds that come from unexpected sources, even friends. In Psalm 55:12–14, David shares how this shook him:

> If an enemy were insulting me, I could endure it; if a foe were raising himself against me, I could hide from him. But it is you, a man like myself, my companion, my close friend, with whom I once enjoyed sweet fellowship as we walked with the throng at the house of God.

It really hurts when your friends (particularly Christian friends) unfairly criticize your efforts to become a healthier, more Christlike woman. But don't let your hurt stop your journey. Keep moving toward your destination.

Sometimes you have to pass slow-moving traffic, just like you might have to pass some of your friends who choose to stay spiritually immature. Outgrowing friends is never easy, but it's going to happen when you choose to grow and they choose to stagnate. You are changing, becoming more like sweet and salty Jesus, and they aren't. You now value the truth—they don't want to hear it. You now make pleasing God your first priority—they want pleasing others to remain your first priority. Gradually, sadly, you just have less and less in common. Keep praying for them, but when God lets you know it's time to move on—move on.

This means that you may have some lonely times on the road to becoming God's Good Woman. It's like when you are driving at night on a crowded highway, and then you slowly pass the pack of cars that surrounds you. Then, before you know it, you are driving in the dark, seemingly alone, with no headlights in your rearview mirror and no taillights up ahead. It's kind of scary to suddenly find yourself alone, but keep your foot on the courage accelerator. There are spiritually mature people up ahead who will become your traveling companions and who will match your spiritual pace.

5. Check for the blue lights before you pull over for the police. Not everyone who pulls you over for a supposed violation on the God's Good Woman journey is legitimate. You are human, you are going to make mistakes, and sometimes you are going to need a correction to get you back on track. If one of God's Good Women or Men gives you a needed rebuke, they won't yell at you or shame you. It's like when a legitimate police officer pulls you over—they won't disrespect or attack you even if you really messed up.

For example, several years ago in December, I (Jennifer) ran a red light and immediately saw the dreaded blue lights flashing. The police officer respectfully told me the particular traffic violation, and asked to see my license and registration. When I told him that I would have to unload my packed car to get the glove box open, he said, "That's not a problem, ma'am, go right ahead." He didn't smirk even once while I unloaded an endless stream of boxes, bags, and cartons, and one enormous, slightly smashed poinsettia. He just wrote me a ticket for $140 (ouch, and right before Christmas!), made sure I could fit everything back in the car, and went on his way. And I haven't run a red light since then—well, maybe a few, but not nearly as many as before.

I needed that respectful, firm rebuke to get me back on track. It hurt me—especially in the wallet—but it didn't permanently harm me. It actually helped me learn to drive more carefully and to remember that careless driving can injure other people. The truth, spoken in love, may hurt you temporarily, but it won't harm you permanently.

I (Paul) have had my share of blue-light-in-the-rearview-mirror moments as well. In college, I was a waiter at a Hilton hotel and showed up very late for work several times in a row due to school obligations. My supervisor's boss, a woman who knew how to be both firm and caring, called me in to her office. She had dealt with many college students before: stressed out, living from pay-check to paycheck, and struggling to make it on their own. I can't remember the exact words she used, but I do remember how she didn't belittle or shame me. She didn't brush my tardiness under the rug, nor did she rub my nose in it. Instead, she did an outstanding job of making my tardiness the problem—not me—and she used the meeting to show me that she cared about my larger dreams and aspirations. I walked out of her office thinking, *This is very strange. I should feel hurt after being corrected by someone. But instead I feel . . . good.* I was blessed by this rebuke from one of God's Good Women who knew she could treat others well as she advanced up the company ladder.

When someone attempts to correct or rebuke you, always check for the blue lights because there are Self-Appointed Deputies of all That is Wrong In the Throng (SADTWITs, for short) who will try to pull you over on your journey and give you a citation. They enjoy pointing out other people's mistakes, real and imaginary. It's their hobby. And unlike the legitimate police officers that God will send your way to deliver a respectful rebuke, the pretend police hand over their citations with a side order of shame, disrespect, and condemnation. You don't have to accept these harmful rebukes. You can ignore their words, change the subject, or even say, "I do not receive that from you."

Freedoms

By now you may be champing at the bit to get in the car and go, but do you have time for one more list? We hope you'll like this list because it proclaims the freedoms that are available to drivers on God's Good Woman Road. You might even want to copy these freedoms and tape them to your dashboard or to someone's forehead for quick reference.

A driver has the freedom to pick who rides shotgun with her. As long as the relationships are beneficial and in line with God's Word, you have the freedom to associate with people of your choice.

A driver has the freedom to say when she needs a break. Some women find it near impossible to rest because they equate taking a break with being selfish. But Jesus sequestered himself from others to get some much needed rest and refreshment. Drivers who push themselves too hard for too long become a hazard to others. You have the freedom (and the responsibility) to rest. So take a nap.

A driver has the freedom to choose the radio station. You are free to ask for and choose what you enjoy and what brings you pleasure, as long as those choices are beneficial and in line with God's Word, and you have listened respectfully to and considered prayerfully what others need (not to be mistaken with what others usually want). This applies at work, play, home, church, in the bedroom, etc.

A driver has the freedom to change lanes or take an alternate route. You have the freedom to change your mind as long as those decisions are beneficial, in line with God's Word, and don't permanently harm the people around you. The decisions you make about your life might hurt other people, but remember, there is a difference between causing someone necessary hurt and causing someone permanent harm. If you suddenly change lanes to avoid an accident, your wise swerve could cause your passengers some temporary hurt, but it would be far worse to stay in that lane and foolishly cause them lasting harm.

For example, a woman might find herself continually overwhelmed, short-tempered, and sharp-tongued because of the competing demands of marriage, motherhood, working outside the home, volunteering at church or school, and running a home. If she stays in that same fast lane, she may end up doing permanent harm to her health and her relationships. She has the freedom (after consulting with God and her family) to change lanes—to make helpful changes in her life such as reducing her number of work hours / stepping completely out of the workforce / hiring a cleaning person / getting off a committee in order to reduce her stress and improve her mood and relationships. This choice may cause hurt temporarily to her workplace or family budget, but it's unlikely to cause permanent damage (harm). On the other hand, if the same overwhelmed woman chose to abandon her family in order to reduce her stress, her unwise choice would permanently harm her husband and kids.

A driver has the freedom to grow spiritually. This freedom, also a responsibility, allows a change in Bible study teachers, denominations, or churches, without finger-pointing or apology.

A driver has the freedom to say no. You are free to say no to an unfair, disrespectful, or dishonest request for your time, talent, or treasure, without an apology or long explanation on your part.

A driver has the freedom not to answer every question. You have the freedom not to provide an answer to every question that comes your way. Jesus didn't answer every question posed to him, and you don't have to either.

Are We There Yet?

When you have left Nice Girl City far behind and are moving into God's Good Woman territory, you'll notice a distinct change in landscape and atmosphere. You won't walk on eggshells anymore, emotionally or spiritually. There's a kind of spiritual ease that will tell you that you are moving in the right direction. You'll have room to stretch and grow, or as Oswald Chambers said, " . . . when God elevates you by his grace into the heavenly places, instead of finding a pinnacle to cling to, you find a great tableland where it is easy to move."[2]

So what are you waiting for? You've got a journey to get started! Crank up the radio—hey, that's Rascal Flatts playing your new theme song: "Life Is a Highway." Roll down the window. Feel the breeze in your hair. And smile . . . a genuine smile that comes from your heart. Feels good, doesn't it?

CNG Nicole

Pulling into the school parking lot, Nicole checks her watch. *Good, I've got ten minutes before Tyler finishes lacrosse practice. I'm going to listen to this new CD and relax.*

As the jazzy sounds of big band music fill the air, she sees Elizabeth crossing the parking lot.

"Hey, Elizabeth!" Nicole rolls down her window and waves. "I didn't know you had a child at this school."

Elizabeth smiles, walking toward Nicole's car. "Yes, we moved into this school district last month. My daughter goes here."

"Is she liking it so far?"

"Yeah, she's adjusting pretty well. She already knew some kids from church that go here, so that helped. Speaking of church, I am really excited about this new mother-daughter ministry idea."

Nodding her agreement, Nicole says, "Me too. I've been doing the same old thing for far too long."

"Good for you for wanting to try something new! We need to stretch ourselves to grow, don't we? It seems like God is—" A loud voice interrupts her next words.

"Nicole, I am so glad to catch you!" Kim, the PTA president, hurries over. "Listen, I know you said that you couldn't return as treasurer for the PTA next year, but no one else has stepped up to volunteer yet. We really need you to serve again."

Oh, great. Now I have to say no again, and in front of Elizabeth too. I hope she won't think I'm not willing to help. "Kim, I just can't do it again. David and I talked and prayed about it, and there are other things we feel led to get involved with instead."

Looking pained, Kim replies, "But you're an accountant. It's a natural fit for you."

Feeling her stomach clench, Nicole thinks, *I am so tired of other people telling me who I am. Lord, I need some help down here. Please help me to be gracious but firm.* "I earn my living as an accountant, but there's more to me than that. I'm glad I could help out this year as treasurer, but I will not be able to do that next year."

Kim sighs. "Okay, I understand. We'll find someone else."

As Kim heads back into the school building, Elizabeth pats Nicole's arm. "Nicely done, Nicole."

Surprised, Nicole glances up. "Really? You thought I handled that well?"

"Absolutely. You were respectful to her, but you also respected what you knew God wanted you to do. It's like my mom always says—'The need is not always the call.' That's a hard lesson to learn sometimes."

Pleased to feel the knots in her stomach unwinding, Nicole adds, "Thanks for those encouraging words, Elizabeth."

"My pleasure. Oh, there's my daughter. Hey, real quick: The first Saturday of next month, I'm having an open house for this ministry that helps persecuted Christian women in third-world countries sell the products they make. If you want, stop by and check out their cute purses and jewelry."

"That's really neat, Elizabeth."

"Well, it's one way to make a difference and help our courageous Christian sisters around the world. I'll e-mail you the details, okay? No pressure to come, just stop by if you can. See you later."

Watching her walk away, Nicole thinks, *Well, how about that, Lord? Thanks for helping me to hold the line with dignity and grace. Oh, and thanks for sending Elizabeth my way. You really do know what I need and just when I need it.*

"Hey, Mom!" Tyler pulls open the car's back door, loading in his lacrosse bag. "Practice was tough today. Coach had us running suicides."

"Suicides? Did you about fall over and die?" asks Nicole as Tyler slides into the front seat.

"No, not until the twentieth one. Me and another boy were the only ones left running." Tyler reaches toward the CD player. "What's this weird music you're listening to? I want to listen to Relient K."

"Not so fast. The driver gets to choose the radio station, or in this case, the CD. When I'm finished listening to this, you can put your CD in. Buckle up."

Clicking his seat belt, Tyler asks, "What kind of music is this?"

"It's called big band music. This particular song is called 'String of Pearls.' My high school jazz band used to play that."

"Did you go hear them play a lot?"

"No, I played saxophone in the jazz band."

Tyler laughs. "Yeah, right. Were you on the karate team too?"

Grinning, Nicole replies, "No, we didn't have a karate team, but I really did play the saxophone."

"That's cool. I never knew you could play an instrument. Were you any good at it?"

Pausing before answering, Nicole thinks, *Usually, I would try to look like a humble Christian and say something that isn't true. This time, instead of giving false humility, which is really a lie in disguise, I want to give an honest answer.* "I was the first chair saxophonist my junior and senior years. I loved playing so much that I practiced all the time."

"Well, if you loved it so much, why'd you stop playing?"

"That, Tyler, is the million-dollar question. It's complicated, but bottom line—I made a bad choice. But everyone makes mistakes, and I've been learning how to make better choices. For example, did you know that your mother the saxophonist is going to audition for the church orchestra next month?"

"Whoa! Mom, you're turning into that Bible woman you were telling me about, what's her name . . . uh, J. Lo?

"J. Lo? You mean Jennifer Lopez?"

"No, I mean that woman who hammered a tent peg into that guy's head."

Dissolving into helpless laughter, Nicole says, "Her name was Jael, not J. Lo. And what does playing the sax have to do with hammering tent pegs into people's heads?"

"Well, J. Lo, or J.L. or whatever her name was, she was brave. I think you're brave for trying out for the orchestra."

Nicole feels warm pleasure spread through her chest. "Thank you, buddy. That means a lot to me."

As she and her son continue their drive home, Nicole reflects on the journey she's been on. *Wow, my own son thinks I'm brave. When was the last time someone told me that? I really am changing, and it feels great. Lord, thanks for showing me how I needed to change to be more like Jesus. Please keep on supplying me with the courage to follow what is more important than my fears. And most of all, thanks for never giving up on the real me. You knew I was in here all along.*

Study Questions

1. Who in your life will be pleased as you journey toward becoming one of God's Good Women? Who will be displeased? How will you handle the positive and negative reactions? How did Jesus handle people who were displeased with his behavior?

2. At this point, what do you think you need to focus more on developing: your courage or your ability to laugh at yourself? What steps could you take to strengthen that quality?

3. Who are your Balcony Women? Take some time to pray and thank the Lord for them. What could you do to express your appreciation to these valued people? If your balcony is empty, what could you do to begin building relationships with potential Balcony Women?

4. Review the potential difficulties that may occur on your journey. Which obstacles are most likely to cause you problems? What can you do now to help you overcome those obstacles in the future?

5. Is there a SADTWIT (see p. 192) in your life who enjoys pointing out your mistakes, real and imaginary? What could you do or say to handle his/her unnecessary rebukes with gracious firmness?

6. Review the freedoms list. Which of these, if you put them into practice immediately, would most benefit your continued spiritual and personal growth?

7. How have you changed as you have studied this book and applied the material to your life? In what way(s) are you more like the 360-degree Jesus today than you were after reading chapter 1?

Bonus Bible Study Question: Read 1 Corinthians 9:24; 2 Corinthians 3:16–18; Galatians 5:7–10; and Hebrews 12:1–3. According to these passages, how should you run your race? What should be your goal? Who and what is waiting for you there?

"Not So Nice" Jesus in the Gospels

The chart on the following pages shows that Jesus wasn't always nice and gentle, but assertive and firm when necessary. Listed are the Gospel passages where we find a more forceful Jesus. Verses in bold print contain the offensive actions of Jesus or the negative reactions or perceptions of others in the listed passage. The number in parentheses is the total number of verses from that passage that speak to the negative action or reaction.

PEOPLE, EVENT, PARABLE, ETC.	MATTHEW	MARK	LUKE	JOHN	NEGATIVE WORDS OR ACTIONS OF JESUS, OR NEGATIVE REACTIONS TO HIM
Visit to Temple at age twelve			2:41–52 vv. **43–44, 48–49** (4)		Jesus did not return home with parents at the appointed time; response to mother when parents found him in the Temple was abrupt and misunderstood by them
Testimony of John the Baptist	3:11–12 v. **12** (1)		3:16–17 v. **17** (1)		John the Baptist warns of impending judgment by Messiah, which was not what the Jews were expecting
First miracle, water made wine				2:1–11 vv. **3–5** (3)	Response to mother's comment is abrupt, and Jesus provided more wine than was needed
Temple cleansed				2:12–25 vv. **15–16, 18–21** (6)	Jesus made whip, drove out money-changers, and expressed righteous anger for how the Temple was being misused—authority is questioned by Jews
Nicodemus' visit				3:1–20 vv. **10–13, 18** (5)	Nicodemus questions Jesus about his teachings

PEOPLE, EVENT, PARABLE, ETC.	MATTHEW	MARK	LUKE	JOHN	NEGATIVE WORDS OR ACTIONS OF JESUS, OR NEGATIVE REACTIONS TO HIM
Rejected at Nazareth			4:16–30 vv. 23–27 (5)		People became furious as he spoke hard truths—was taken to the edge of town where they intended to throw him over a cliff, but he walked away
Beatitudes	5:3–12 vv. 11–12 (2)		6:20–26 vv. 22, 24–26 (4)		Words that contrast spiritual values with worldly values and the persecution, insults, etc., that will come to followers of Christ
Teaching about the law	5:17–20 v. 20 (1)				Forceful truth concerning righteousness and entering the kingdom of heaven
Teaching about anger	5:21–26 v. 22 (1)				Words of truth concerning anger by making things right with others before a person loses control and becomes subject to God's judgment
Teaching about lust	5:27–30 vv. 29–30 (2)				Words of warning that sin should not be tolerated in a person's life
Teaching about vows	5:37 v. 37 (1)				Words emphasizing the importance of speaking the truth

PEOPLE, EVENT, PAR-ABLE, ETC.	MATTHEW	MARK	LUKE	JOHN	NEGATIVE WORDS OR ACTIONS OF JESUS, OR NEGATIVE REACTIONS TO HIM
Teaching about forgiveness	6:14–15 v. 15 (1)				Warning that those who don't forgive won't be forgiven by God
Teaching about criticizing others	7:1–5 vv. 1–5 (5)		6:37–42 vv. 41–42 (2)		Stern warning against having a hypocritical, judgmental attitude
Narrow and broad gates	7:13–14 vv. 13–14 (2)				Truth about the only way to eternal life
Fruit in people's lives	7:15–20 v. 19 (1)		6:43–45 vv. 43–45 (3)		Warning to examine "fruit" produced by others—deliberately teaching false doctrine produces "bad fruit" and judgment—reminder that a deceptive heart will be revealed in one's speech and behavior
Judgment of the "religious"	7:21–23 vv. 21, 23 (2)		6:46 v. 46 (1)		Sober warning against those who sound "religious" but have no personal relationship with him
Wise and foolish builders	7:24–27 vv. 26–27 (2)		6:47–49 v. 49 (1)		Warning to those who hear his words and don't put them into practice

PEOPLE, EVENT, PARABLE, ETC.	MATTHEW	MARK	LUKE	JOHN	NEGATIVE WORDS OR ACTIONS OF JESUS, OR NEGATIVE REACTIONS TO HIM
Reaction to Jesus' claim to be Son of God				5:16–47 vv. 16, 18–47 (31)	Jews persecuted Jesus and tried harder to kill him because of claim he made to be Son of God—Jesus rebukes them for their unbelief
Jesus rebukes disciples			9:51–56 v. 55 (1)		Jesus rebukes James and John for asking if they should call fire down on those who didn't welcome him
Cost of following Jesus	8:18–22 v. 22 (1)		9:57–62 vv. 60, 62 (2)		Jesus shares hard truths about total dedication versus halfhearted commitment
Calming the storm	8:23–27 vv. 24, 26 (2)	4:35–41 vv. 38, 41 (2)	8:22–25 vv. 23, 25 (2)		After leaving the crowds behind, Jesus fell asleep (a human need) in the boat—awakened by disciples—calmed storm—disciples amazed and fearful
Sending demons into pigs	8:28–34 vv. 32, 34 (2)	5:1–20 vv. 13, 15, 17 (3)	8:26–37 vv. 33, 37 (2)		People were fearful of Jesus' supernatural power and upset at losing herd of pigs—pleaded with Jesus to leave their area

PEOPLE, EVENT, PARABLE, ETC.	MATTHEW	MARK	LUKE	JOHN	NEGATIVE WORDS OR ACTIONS OF JESUS, OR NEGATIVE REACTIONS TO HIM
Eating with sinners	9:10–13 vv. 11–13 (3)	2:13–17 vv. 16–17 (2)	5:27–32 vv. 30–32 (3)		Scribes and Pharisees question why Jesus eats with "sinners," and he exposes their self-righteousness
Healing of blind and mute	9:27–34 vv. 30, 34 (2)				Stern warning from Jesus not to share what had happened, and Pharisees accuse him of driving out demons by prince of demons
Sending out of twelve disciples	10:5–16 vv. 5, 14–15 (3)	Mark 6:8–11 v. 11 (1)	Luke 9:3–5 v. 5 (1)		Disciples instructed to go only to Jews and to separate themselves from those who rejected them
Preparation for persecution	10:17–39 vv. 17–18, 21–22, 32–39 (12)				Words of instruction on how to deal with persecution and making God one's first priority no matter the cost
Challenge to his generation	11:16–19 vv. 16–19 (4)				Words of rebuke to his generation that no matter what he said or did, they were cynical and skeptical—didn't want their comfortable, self-centered lives to be challenged

PEOPLE, EVENT, PARABLE, ETC.	MATTHEW	MARK	LUKE	JOHN	NEGATIVE WORDS OR ACTIONS OF JESUS, OR NEGATIVE REACTIONS TO HIM
Lack of repentance	11:20–24 vv. 21–24 (4)				Harsh words concerning judgment for those who fail to repent
Disciples pick wheat on Sabbath	12:1–8 vv. 3–8 (6)	2:23–28 vv. 25–28 (4)	6:1–5 vv. 3–5 (3)		Challenge to Pharisees and their interpretation of the Law—a little sarcasm when Jesus asks them if they had even read the Law
Healing on the Sabbath	12:9–14 vv. 11–12, 14 (3)	3:1–6 vv. 2, 4–6 (4)	6:6–11 vv. 7, 9, 11 (3)		Ridicule of Pharisees' petty rules and loyalty to "religious" system, exposing their evil attitudes before entire synagogue—Pharisees plot Jesus' murder
Crowds follow Jesus	12:15–16 v. 16 (1)	3:7–12 vv. 9, 12 (2)			Withdraws to keep crowd from touching him and gave strict orders not to tell who he was
Accusation of religious leaders	12:24–37 vv. 25–37 (13)	3:22–30 vv. 23–29 (7)			Stern warning concerning the unpardonable sin and the day of judgment—harsh words for the Pharisees

PEOPLE, EVENT, PARABLE, ETC.	MATTHEW	MARK	LUKE	JOHN	NEGATIVE WORDS OR ACTIONS OF JESUS, OR NEGATIVE REACTIONS TO HIM
Religious leaders ask for miracle	12:38–45 vv. 39–45 (7)				Confronts Pharisees concerning their rejection of miracles and truth already revealed to them—condemnation for "a wicked and adulterous generation"
True family	12:46–50 v. 48 (1)	3:31–35 v. 33 (1)	8:19–21 v. 21 (1)		Rejects earthly family
Parables of weeds and fishing net	13:24–30, 36–42, 47–50 vv. 40–42, 49–50 (5)				Strong words concerning the end of the age, and judgment of righteous and wicked
People of Nazareth refuse to believe	13:53–58 v. 57 (1)	6:1–6 vv. 3–4 (2)			People were amazed and offended by this "hometown" man and his claims
Need for solitude	14:6–13 v. 13 (1)	6:21–32 vv. 31–32 (2)			Need to withdraw from crowds for rest and quiet after receiving news of death of John the Baptist
Jesus walks on water	14:22–33 vv. 26, 31 (2)	6:45–52 vv. 49–50 (2)		6:16–21 v. 19 (1)	Disciples were terrified when they saw Jesus walking on the water—thought he was a ghost

PEOPLE, EVENT, PARABLE, ETC.	MATTHEW	MARK	LUKE	JOHN	NEGATIVE WORDS OR ACTIONS OF JESUS, OR NEGATIVE REACTIONS TO HIM
Jews disagree and many disciples desert				6:22–66 vv. 26–66 (41)	Jews disagree with Jesus over his hard teachings—he rebukes them, and many of his disciples desert him
Ridiculed by brothers				7:1–9 vv. 3–8 (6)	Brothers challenge Jesus to reveal himself to the world—didn't believe in him
Jesus teaches in Temple				7:10–52 vv. 12, 15, 16–30 (17)	People accuse Jesus of being a deceiver—amazed at his teachings but think he is demon-possessed and try to seize him
Forgiveness for adulterous woman				8:1–11 vv. 3–7 (5)	Pharisees try to set a trap in order to accuse Jesus
Challenge by Pharisees and the Jews				8:12–59 vv. 13–19, 21–29, 33–59 (43)	Pharisees challenge the validity of his testimony—Jesus rebukes the Jews because they are ready to kill him—Jews accuse him of being demon-possessed and pick up stones to stone him

PEOPLE, EVENT, PARABLE, ETC.	MATTHEW	MARK	LUKE	JOHN	NEGATIVE WORDS OR ACTIONS OF JESUS, OR NEGATIVE REACTIONS TO HIM
Jesus heals blind man				9:1–41 vv. **16, 22, 29–34, 41** (9)	Pharisees become very upset when man healed of blindness tells them what Jesus did for him—deny even knowing where Jesus comes from
The good shepherd				10:11–20 vv. **19–20** (2)	As Jesus teaches, people are divided and accuse him of being demon-possessed and insane
In the Temple				10:22–39 vv. **25–39** (15)	Jews accuse Jesus of blasphemy and try to stone him
Death of Lazarus				11:1–44 v. **6** (1)	Jesus did not come when he heard Lazarus was sick, but delayed his arrival for two more days
Religious leaders plot to kill Jesus				11:46–57 vv. **53, 57** (2)	Sanhedrin plots to arrest Jesus and kill him
Many unbelievers				12:37–43 v. **42** (1)	Even after all the miraculous signs, many people did not believe—some believers would not confess their faith for fear they would be put out of the synagogue—loved praise of men more than praise from God

PEOPLE, EVENT, PARABLE, ETC.	MATTHEW	MARK	LUKE	JOHN	NEGATIVE WORDS OR ACTIONS OF JESUS, OR NEGATIVE REACTIONS TO HIM
Clean and unclean	15:1-20 vv. 3-9, 12-14 (10)	7:5-23 vv. 6-13 (8)			Harsh criticism of the hypocritical Pharisees, which offends them
Syrophoenician woman	15:21-28 vv. 23-24, 26 (3)	7:24-30 v. 27 (1)			Ignores woman and then gives reasons not to grant her request
Asking for sign in sky	16:1-4 vv. 2-4 (3)	8:11-12 v. 12 (1)			Refuses to grant sign because it would still not be adequate to convince the religious leaders he was the Messiah
Yeast of Pharisees	16:5-12 vv. 8-11 (4)	8:13-21 vv. 17-19, 21 (4)			Confronts disciples about their faith and lack of understanding
Rebuke of Peter	16:21-23 v. 23 (1)	8:31-34 v. 33 (1)			Rebukes Peter with very stern words
Healing of demon-possessed boy	17:14-18 v. 17 (1)	9:15-27 v. 19 (1)	9:38-43 v. 41 (1)		Rebukes disciples who are unable to heal boy—frustrated with "unbelieving and perverse generation"
Causing others to sin	18:1-9 vv. 6-9 (4)	9:42-48 vv. 42-48 (7)			Strong warning concerning causing others to sin and the resulting judgment

PEOPLE, EVENT, PARABLE, ETC.	MATTHEW	MARK	LUKE	JOHN	NEGATIVE WORDS OR ACTIONS OF JESUS, OR NEGATIVE REACTIONS TO HIM
Sending out messengers			10:1–16 vv. 10–16 (7)		Messengers receive strong words from Jesus concerning how to react to people who reject them
Jesus visits Mary and Martha			10:38–42 vv. 40–42 (3)		Martha is distracted, worried, and upset and appeals to Jesus, who teaches her about a better way
Jesus answers hostile accusations			11:14–26 vv. 14–26 (13)		Crowd is amazed and accuses Jesus of driving out demons by Beelzebub—asks for sign from heaven
Criticism of religious leaders			11:37–53 vv. 38–53 (16)		Jesus invited to dine with Pharisee but surprises him by not washing before the meal—Jesus issues a very stern rebuke, which the people saw as an insult and they begin to oppose him and besiege him with questions
Speaking against hypocrisy			12:1–11 vv. 1–5, 9–10 (7)		Jesus warns against the yeast of the Pharisees, which is hypocrisy

PEOPLE, EVENT, PARABLE, ETC.	MATTHEW	MARK	LUKE	JOHN	NEGATIVE WORDS OR ACTIONS OF JESUS, OR NEGATIVE REACTIONS TO HIM
Healing of crippled woman			13:10–17 vv. 14-17 (4)		Synagogue ruler was indignant because Jesus healed on the Sabbath—Jesus issues scathing response and humiliates his opponents
Accusation from Pharisees			15:1–2; 16:14–17 vv. 15:2; 16:14–17 (5)		Pharisees mutter against Jesus because he welcomed sinners and ate with them—sneered at Jesus because they loved money
Rich young ruler	19:16–24 vv. 17, 21, 23–24 (4)	10:17–25 vv. 18, 21, 23–25 (5)	18:18–25 vv. 22, 24–25 (3)		Truth spoken to young man caused him to be sad and turn away from Jesus
Second cleansing of Temple	21:12–13 vv. 12–13 (2)	11:15–18 vv. 15–17 (3)	19:45–46 vv. 45–46 (2)		Drives out buyers and sellers, over-turns tables, speaks harsh rebuke to "den of thieves"
Religious leaders challenge Jesus' authority	21:23–32 vv. 24, 27, 31–32 (4)	11:27–33 vv. 29–30, 33 (3)	20:1–8 vv. 3, 8 (2)		Firmly exposes motives of leaders, and their trap ("trick question") is avoided
Paying taxes	22:15–22 vv. 18–21 (4)	12:13–17 vv. 15–17 (3)	20:20–26 vv. 23–25 (3)		Hypocrisy of Pharisees exposed as they try to trap Jesus by his words

PEOPLE, EVENT, PARABLE, ETC.	MATTHEW	MARK	LUKE	JOHN	NEGATIVE WORDS OR ACTIONS OF JESUS, OR NEGATIVE REACTIONS TO HIM
Sadducees question about resurrection	22:23–33 vv. 29–32 (4)	12:18–27 vv. 24–27 (4)	20:27–40 vv. 34–36 (3)		Direct, strong answer that astonished and silenced the people
Condemnation of religious leaders	23:1–36 vv. 3–36 (34)	12:38–40 vv. 38–40 (3)	20:46–47 vv. 46–47 (2)		Scathing condemnation of the behavior and hypocrisy of the religious leaders
Speaking of the future and his return	24:3–51 vv. 4–51 (48)	13:4–37 vv. 5–37 (33)	21:7–36 vv. 8–36 (29)		Warning concerning being deceived by false prophets, and revolutionary, shocking truths concerning the end of the age, Christ's return, and remaining watchful
Final Judgment	25:1–46 vv. 11–13, 29–30, 32–33, 41–46 (13)				Rejection of unbelievers and eternal punishment meted out in hell
Woman anoints Jesus	26:6–13 vv. 8–10 (3)	14:3–9 vv. 5–6 (2)		12:3–8 v. 7 (1)	Defense of woman's action of using the expensive perfume in the face of the indignation of the disciples
Betrayal	26:20–26 vv. 21, 23–25 (4)	14:18–21 vv. 18, 20–21 (3)	22:21–22 vv. 21–22 (2)	13:21–28 vv. 21, 26–27 (3)	Shocking revelation to the disciples that one of them would betray Jesus

PEOPLE, EVENT, PARABLE, ETC.	MATTHEW	MARK	LUKE	JOHN	NEGATIVE WORDS OR ACTIONS OF JESUS, OR NEGATIVE REACTIONS TO HIM
Peter's denial predicted	26:31–35 vv. **31, 34** (2)	14:27–31 vv. **27, 30** (2)	22:33–34 v. **34** (1)		Hard truth that not only would Peter deny Jesus, but the other disciples would also desert him—assertion by Peter this would never happen
Agony in the garden of Gethsemane	26:36–46 vv. **36–42, 45** (8)	14:32–42 vv. **32–38, 41** (8)	22:40–46 vv. **40–42, 44–46** (6)		In his humanity, troubled, distressed, and overwhelmed with sorrow—needed support and prayers of disciples who were asleep—willing to be obedient to Father's will
Rebukes Peter for using his sword	26:47–56 vv. **52–54** (3)		22:35–38, 47–54 v. **51** (1)	18:1–14 v. **11** (1)	After telling the disciples to buy a sword if they don't have one, Jesus rebukes Peter when Peter tries to defend Jesus and cuts off the high priest's servant's ear.
Before the Sanhedrin	26:59–66 v. **64** (1)	14:55–64 v. **62** (1)			With calmness and courage, Jesus declares he is the Messiah even though it meant his death—accused of blasphemy, and Sanhedrin condemned him as worthy of death

PEOPLE, EVENT, PARABLE, ETC.	MATTHEW	MARK	LUKE	JOHN	NEGATIVE WORDS OR ACTIONS OF JESUS, OR NEGATIVE REACTIONS TO HIM
Jesus before Pilate	27:11–14 vv. 11–12 (2)	15:1–5 v. 2 (1)	23:1–5 v. 3 (1)	18:28–38 vv. 34, 36–37 (3)	Pilate is amazed that Jesus does not try to defend himself against accusations he knows are untrue
Jesus appears to disciples		16:14 v. 14 (1)		20:24–30 v. 27 (1)	Jesus rebuked disciples for their lack of faith
Jesus talks with Peter				21:15–25 v. 17 (1)	Peter's feelings are hurt when Jesus questions him a third time about his love for the Lord
Great Commission	28:16–20 v. 17 (1)	16:15–16 v. 16 (1)			Those who don't believe are condemned

Number of verses in four gospels   3,779

Verses with negative reactions/perceptions   733

Percentage of four gospels   19.4%

Abuse in Marriage

If you are in a physically abusive relationship or feel at all endangered, get out NOW. For assistance, call the National Domestic Violence Hotline at 1-800-799-SAFE(7233) or TTY 1-800-787-3224, 24 hours a day, 365 days a year. Hotline advocates are available for victims and anyone calling on their behalf to provide crisis intervention, safety planning, information, and referrals to agencies in all fifty states, Puerto Rico, and the U.S. Virgin Islands. Assistance is available in English and Spanish with access to more than 170 languages through interpreter services. For more information, go online to *www.ndvh.org*.

Whether the abuse is physical or emotional, Christian Nice Wives may take years to recognize that what they are experiencing in their marriage is, in fact, abusive. Emotional and spiritual abuse can be verbal or nonverbal, but its aim is the same as physical abuse: to chip away at your self-worth and independence. Examples of abuse include:

- Verbal and emotional abuse, such as countering and correcting most of what you say, discounting your opinions and comments, name-calling, interrogating, mocking, accusing/blaming, trivializing your experiences, giving you the silent treatment or cold shoulder, undermining your efforts, shaming, ordering you around, yelling, cursing, raging, making threats, "forgetting" or denying past abuse, isolating you from family and friends, taking away the phone or car, or interfering intentionally with your sleep.

- Physical intimidation, such as slamming doors, backing you up against a wall or in a corner, blocking your exit through a door, or pounding or breaking things.
- Physical violence, such as pinching, tripping, spitting, poking, shoving, slapping, punching, kicking, strangling, pushing you down, forcing you to have sex, or throwing things at or near you.[1]

When abused Christian Nice Wives finally recognize what's going on in their marriages, their next question is often, "But don't you believe in the power of God to change him?" The answer is yes, God is powerful enough to change him, but in the Bible, neither God nor Jesus went around healing people willy-nilly. Whoever wanted to be changed had to cooperate in the process, and many times had to ask directly for what they wanted.

For example, in Mark 10, Jesus asks blind Bartimaeus, "What do you want me to do for you?" (v. 51). Shouldn't that have been obvious? The man was blind. He probably wasn't approaching Jesus to ask if he knew the way to San Jose. Jesus already had a good idea what this man wanted from him. So why did he ask? Because Jesus wanted that man to be aware of his own need for change and to cooperate in his own healing before Jesus would do anything for him. So many Christian Nice Girls date, marry, and stay with emotionally damaged, abusive men because these women are holding on to the false belief that someday God is going "to get a hold of" and magically change him. Sometimes women look at the apostle Paul's Damascus Road experience and hope that Jesus will do that for their man; however,

God had to physically blind Paul to get him to see how spiritually blind he was to his own abusiveness. Paul could have ignored this experience or become bitter about it, but instead he cooperated with what happened to him. He listened and participated in his own healing.

If you are dating or are married to an abusive man and want him to change, please consider that instead of praying for God to miraculously develop empathy and emotional maturity in him, you should pray for the mighty right arm of the Lord to move and afflict your man to such a degree that he is painfully humbled like the apostle Paul. He was an arrogant, self-righteous, abusive man until God struck him down publicly. God made Paul desperate, and as testimony after testimony shows, many people will only change due to desperation as opposed to inspiration. Christian Nice Girlfriends and Wives hold out for inspiration, partly because it requires no work on their part. They don't have to make tough relationship decisions. CNGirlfriends and Wives don't want to risk the conflict that their decisions might bring them, so they hide behind the possibility of a highly improbable miracle.

Please, if you suspect that you are in an abusive relationship, seek help from a qualified counselor who understands what verbal and emotional abuse look like. Some counselors are trained to recognize signs of physical abuse but are not familiar with the psychological warfare women can experience from verbal, emotional, or spiritual abuse. *The Emotionally Destructive Relationship* by Christian counselor Leslie Vernick is an excellent resource for believers and provides wise, biblically sound advice on dealing with abusive spouses, parents, and friends. Patricia Evans has written several good books on verbal/emotional abuse, including *The Verbally Abusive Relationship* and *The Verbally Abusive Man: Can He Change?* If you have experienced physical abuse, Lundy Bancroft's *Why Does He Do That? Inside the Minds of Angry and Controlling Men* is a powerful, eye-opening book written by a counselor with many years of experience working with abusive men.

Evans' and Bancroft's books are not specifically Christian resources, but they contain valuable information nonetheless.

One final note: If you know that you would have to hide the above books from your husband or boyfriend while you read them because you are afraid of his reaction, then there is a very good chance that you are in an abusive relationship.

Notes

Introduction

1. If you are thinking, *This sounds just like my husband, brother, father, etc.*, take a look at Paul's book *No More Christian Nice Guy: When Being Nice—Instead of Good—Hurts Men, Women, and Children*. While *No More Christian Nice Guy* and *No More Christian Nice Girl* cover some similar material, they also address issues and situations that are unique to each gender and are written with distinctly male or female perspectives.

Chapter 1

1. Statistics compiled by Rebecca A. Mackey. For a list of gospel verses showing Jesus' firm and forceful side, see appendix A.
2. Salt Association, "About Salt," *www.saltsense.co.uk/aboutsalt-facts01.htm*
3. Matthew George Easton, *The Bible Dictionary: Your Biblical Reference Book* (Charleston, SC: Forgotten Books, 2007), 272.
4. David Murrow, *Why Men Hate Going to Church* (Nashville, TN: Thomas Nelson, 2005), 70–71.

Chapter 2

1. "Knew Coke," *www.snopes.com/cokelore/newcoke.asp*.
2. Anne Moir and David Jessel, *Brain Sex: The Real Difference Between Men and Women* (New York: Dell, 1992), 46–48.
3. Ibid.
4. "Human Brain (Anatomy): The Limbic System," *www.brainanatomy.net/str9.html*.
5. S. E. Taylor, L. C. Klein, B. P. Lewis, T. L. Gruenewald, R. A. R. Gurung, and J. A. Updegraff, "Biobehavioral Responses to Stress in Females: Tend-and-Befriend, not Fight-or-Flight," *Psychological Review* 107 (2000): 411–429.

6. Moir and Jessel, 48.
7. Frans de Waal, *Peacemaking Among the Primates* (Cambridge, MA: Harvard University Press, 1989), 121.
8. Sandy Sheehy, *Connecting: The Enduring Power of Female Friendship* (New York: William Morrow, 2000), 82–83.
9. "Hormone Involved in Reproduction May Have Role in the Maintenance of Relationships," July 14, 1999, *www.oxytocin.org/oxytoc/*.
10. Taylor, Klein, Lewis, Gruenewald, Gurung, and Updegraff.
11. Carol L. Philpot, Gary R. Brooks, Don-David Lusterman, Roberta L. Nutt, *Bridging Separate Gender Worlds: Why Men and Women Clash and How Therapists Can Bring Them Together* (Washington, DC: American Psychological Association, 1997), 35–65.
12. D. C. Carter, *Current Conceptions of Sex Roles and Sex Typing: Theory and Research* (New York: Praeger, 1987).
13. C. P. Edwards, "Behavioral Sex Differences in Children of Diverse Cultures: The Case of Nurturance to Infants" in M. Pereira and L. Fairbanks, eds., *Juveniles: Comparative Socioecology* (Oxford: Oxford University Press, 1991), 195.
14. *How Schools Shortchange Girls: The AAUW Report: A Study of Major Findings on Girls and Education* (New York: Marlowe & Co., 1995), 149.
15. D. Reay, " 'Spice Girls,' 'Nice Girls,' 'Girlies,' and 'Tomboys': Gender Discourses, Girls' Cultures and Femininities in the Primary Classroom," *Gender and Education* 13, no. 2 (2001): 153–166.
16. A. P. Davis and T. R. McDaniel, "You've Come a Long Way, Baby—Or Have You? Research Evaluating Gender Portrayal in Recent Caldecott-Winning Books," *The Reading Teacher* 52 (1999): 532–536.
17. P. Purcell and L. Stewart, "Dick and Jane in 1989," *Sex Roles* 22 (1990): 177–185.
18. *How Schools Shortchange Girls.*
19. Edward B. Fiske, "Lessons: Even at a Former Women's College, Male Students Are Taken More Seriously, A Researcher Finds," *New York Times*, April 11, 1990, national edition, Living Arts Section.
20. D. Roberts, U. Foehr, and V. Rideout, *Generation M: Media in the Lives of 8- to 18-Year-Olds*, *http://kff.org/entmedia/mh012010pkg.cfm*.
21. "Reflections of Girls in the Media, A Report on the Fourth Annual Children and the Media Conference," *http://publications.childrennow.org/assets/pdf/cmp/reflections/reflections-girls-media.pdf.*
22. Lyn Mikel Brown, *Girlfighting: Betrayal and Rejection Among Girls* (New York: New York University Press, 2003), 21.
23. J. Kelly and S. L. Smith, "Where the Girls Aren't: Gender Disparity Satu-

rates G-rated Films" [Research brief] (2006). Retrieved June 13, 2009, from *www.seejane.org.*

24. Girls, Women & Media Project, "Fewer Female Characters/Roles in Entertainment Media," *www.mediaandwomen.org/problem3.html.*

25. P. A. Adler, S. J. Kless, and P. Adler, "Socialization to Gender Roles: Popularity Among Elementary School Boys and Girls," *Sociology of Education* 65 (1992): 169–187.

26. Lyn Mikel Brown, 206.

27. Cheryl Dellasega and Charisse Nixon, *Girl Wars: 12 Strategies That Will End Female Bullying* (New York: Fireside, 2003), 2.

28. As a crusader against adolescent bullying, Paul combats the role that impossible beauty standards play in girl-on-girl aggression by hanging on his family's refrigerator door photos of celebrities without makeup. We recommend that other parents do the same to expose how airbrushed photos deceive, and to help daughters out of this false economy that equates worth primarily with beauty.

29. Lyn Mikel Brown, 32.

30. Ibid., 49–50.

31. Ibid., 53.

Chapter 3

1. Martin H. Teicher, Susan L. Andersen, Ann Polcari, Carl M. Anderson, Carryl P. Navalta, and Dennis M. Kim, "The Neurobiological Consequences of Early Stress and Childhood Maltreatment," *Neuroscience & Biobehavioral Reviews* 27, Issues 1–2 (January to March 2003): 33–44.

Chapter 4

1. Paul J. Achtemeier, *Harper's Bible Dictionary,* 1st ed. (San Francisco: Harper & Row, 1985), S. 214; Matthew Henry, *Matthew Henry's Commentary on the Whole Bible: Complete and Unabridged in One Volume* (Peabody, MA: Hendrickson, 1996, c1991), S. Judg. 4:4.

2. D. A. Carson, *New Bible Commentary: 21st Century Edition,* 4th ed. (Leicester, England; Downers Grove, IL: InterVarsity Press, 1994), S. Acts 16:11. As for urging them to stay with her, see Matthew Henry, S. Acts 16:6; Robert Jamieson, A. R. Fausset, David Brown, *A Commentary, Critical and Explanatory, on the Old and New Testaments* (Oak Harbor, WA: Logos Research Systems, Inc., 1997), S. Acts 16:15; Warren W. Wiersbe, *The Bible Exposition Commentary* (Wheaton, IL: Victor Books, 1996, c1989), S. Acts 16:6.

3. John MacArthur, *Different by Design* (Wheaton, IL: Victor Books, 1994), 135.

4. Larry Richards, *The Bible Reader's Companion* (Wheaton, IL: Victor Books, 1991), S. 752; Robert Jamieson, A. R. Fausset, and David Brown,

A Commentary, Critical and Explanatory, on the Old and New Testaments (Oak Harbor, WA: Logos Research Systems, Inc., 1997), S. Rom. 16:3; Craig S. Keener, *The IVP Bible Background Commentary: New Testament* (Downers Grove, IL: InterVarsity Press, 1993), S. Rom. 16:2–3.

5. Ace Collins, *Stories Behind Women of Extraordinary Faith* (Grand Rapids, MI: Zondervan, 2008), 69–70.

6. Margaret Washington, *Sojourner Truth's America* (Chicago: University of Illinois Press, 2009), 378.

Chapter 7

1. "The Amazing Story of Kudzu," *www.maxshores.com/kudzu/.*

Chapter 8

1. Tommy Nelson, *The Book of Romance* (Nashville, TN: Thomas Nelson, 1998), xiii.

Chapter 9

1. Lois P. Frankel, *Nice Girls Don't Get the Corner Office: 101 Unconscious Mistakes Women Make That Sabotage Their Careers* (New York: Time Warner, 2004), 26–27.

2. Ibid., 70–71.

3. Ibid., 54.

4. Ibid., 68.

5. Pat Heim, Susan Murphy, and Susan Golant, *In the Company of Women: Indirect Aggression Among Women: Why We Hurt Each Other and How to Stop* (New York: Tarcher/Putnam, 2001), 144–149.

6. Ibid., 26.

7. Ibid., 152.

8. Ibid., 27.

Chapter 10

1. Sandy has these lessons available for other moms who want to bring Balcony Girls into the lives of their daughters. You can learn more at her Web site: *www.reluctantentertainer.com.*

2. Oswald Chambers, *My Utmost for His Highest* (Grand Rapids, MI: Discovery House Publishers, 1963), March 27 reading.

Appendix B

1. Patricia Evans, *The Verbally Abusive Man: Can He Change? A Woman's Guide to Deciding Whether to Stay or Go* (Avon, MA: Adams Media, 2006).